STUMBLING
Toward the
Buddha

STUMBLING
Toward the
Buddha

**Stories about Tripping over My Principles
on the Road to Transformation**

Dawn Downey

Pathless Land Press
Kansas City MO

Copyright © 2014 by Dawn Downey
All rights reserved.

Published 2014 by Pathless Land Press
Printed in the United States of America
18 17 16 15 14   1 2 3 4 5
ISBN 978-0-692026-39-7
Library of Congress Control Number: 2014907516

Cover design by Teresa Mandala of Bella Designs
Author photo by Stephen Locke

For Ben, my big sweetie.

Table of Contents

Part I
Nobody's Perfect: Accepting My Humanity

The Collection 3

The Price: Desire is More than I Bargained For 8

Freeways, Foothills, and Phobias: Courage
Takes a Sunday Drive 13

Attachments: I Can't Let Go, Despite the Wisdom of
Nonattachment 19

Mirror, Mirror: What, Me Prejudiced? 31

Part II
Bad Things Happen to Good People—If They're Lucky: Transcending Difficulties

Alone in the Dark: Meditating at a
War-Torn Peace Rally 39

Fun and Games 43

The *N* Word: A Prayer of Thanksgiving 51

Anicca: How I Escaped from Maniacal Meditators . . . 57

Burgers, Beer, and Emotional Baggage:
Marinate in Mindfulness before Grilling Yourself . . . 67

Truth Transcends the Facts: A Hoax Unveils
the Nature of Reality 74

Part III
Revelations: Finding Myself
Toadstools: Fighting Depression, Defending the Lawn . . 83

The Doll House 89

Part IV
Oneness Makes Strange Bedfellows: Losing My Self
Clear Comprehension without Delusion 103

No Longer Mother 107

Call to Prayer 109

Blurred Edges 114

Palin Power: On Discovering the
Emptiness of Knowledge 117

Precious Moments 124

Part V
A Question a Day Keeps the Answers Away: Making Peace with Paradox
Paradise 133

The Road to Transformation 138

Resurrection: Birth and Death Right Now 140

The Inheritance 145

Light and Shadow 154

About the Author 169

Acknowledgments 171

Stumbling Toward the Buddha

Part I
Nobody's Perfect:
Accepting My Humanity

When an upscale lifestyle magazine featured a friend's Los Angeles home, it was a sixteen-page, full-color spread of my jealousy. The green-eyed monster drooled all over her Ming porcelain. It hunkered down on her French settee. What is a settee, anyway? I plunged elbow deep into the horse manure of envy in order to recover my former affection, then emailed her a cheery congratulation. She responded in half an hour. "BTW," she said, "I love your blog." Oh. My words were her treasures, perhaps displayed on her turn-of-the-century Rococo game table. Elegantly backlit, because, after all, she has exquisite taste.

The Collection

My personal treasures make the acquisitions of the Smithsonian look like tchotchkes. The holdings of the Louvre are mere keepsakes in comparison, King Tut's treasures cheap trinkets. I've amassed a collection mined from the caverns of memory, a museum filled with priceless gems—my thoughts.

Humdrum Hall stores workhorse thoughts. Not very pretty, but always close by when needed. To your right, at the bottom of the laundry basket: *Wish these clothes would wash themselves for a change.* In front of the television: *Shoot, too cold to go for a walk today—but on the bright side, too cold to weed the garden.* Please hold your noses, before I open the refrigerator door for: *Oh no, another bowl of green fuzz.*

Follow me up the down escalator to Fantasy Foyer, where the tooth fairy supervises acquisitions. Note the funhouse mirrors. I'm particularly proud of beauties like: *After I lose five pounds, my little black dress will fit again,* and *Don't care what anybody says, gold lamé clogs are right in style.* Keep a safe distance from: *I'll clean out the closet next week,* or you'll get cobwebs in your hair.

Single file, please. The hallway narrows as it winds around to Beliefs Atrium. B.A. requires specialized ventilation, because its contents are ancient and fragile. Don't be alarmed—the door will close behind you with a vacuum seal, which keeps out fresh air. Space is limited; there's no room for newer models, as long as these crowd every corner. Let's pause to reflect on *I need to meditate twice a day*, picked up at a Buddhist monastery. The viewpoint under the American flag is on a four-year rotation: *My political party won't mess things up like the other guys.*

Maintenance costs in Beliefs Atrium eclipse those in other areas of the museum. I squandered thirty-three years on the upkeep of: *A traditional career path will lead to success and happiness.*

Try harder and this marriage will work. Eighteen years.

Just five little pounds, just five. Well... five years.

Wear clean underwear in case you get into an accident. Half a century and counting.

We're now approaching Dawn Salon, which houses the most rare thoughts of all. You can't purchase these jewels anywhere else. In the doorway: *My name is Dawn.* A perfection of simplicity, don't you think? Turn your attention toward something more complex, the mobile overhead: *I resigned from a secure position, with $20,000 to my name, to gamble on a writing career.* Shifting air currents alternately show off its polished surfaces, then accentuate its shadows. And one more, just to give you a flavor of the whole Dawn series: *I'm middle-aged, with a house and a mortgage.* Not attractive by traditional standards, but integral to the set.

According to provenance, each piece originated right here. But a woman out in California, a fellow attendee at a writers' conference, claimed her name was also Dawn (now appended as The Younger, for purposes of differentiation). Not only that, every thought in the Salon described her life as well as mine. Coincidence? Hardly. She obviously bought them from a forger. God forbid, she owns the originals and mine are the fakes.

Now, on to Ornery Alcove. Be careful. Mental activity is quite unstable in this area. Jokes leap from pedestals at the slightest provocation.

To set the mood before his dharma talk, our meditation teacher introduced it with an instruction. "Please listen in a meditative frame of mind."

A resident of Ornery Alcove pounced: *Well, I'm not going to.*

The teacher couldn't possibly have heard, but he did glance in my direction before he continued. "The Buddha discovered 102 forms of consciousness. How many do you experience in your life?"

104, what's it to ya?

We'd better leave before someone gets hurt. Young lady on the cell phone, pay attention. *Let's pretend there's a spider* is about to crawl up your leg.

Heading over to Doubt District. Please put on your night-vision goggles for this section of the tour. The lights short out constantly. Careful you don't trip over *Who are you kidding? That black dress will never fit again.*

Dawn The Younger (sneaking around in my museum again) asked me to suggest a title for an article she'd written. A dozen suggestions came to mind, rolled out like an assembly line... that is, until volunteers from Doubt District slowed down the process. You can see them crouched in the far corner: *God, these titles are corny. Boy, do these need help. That one's really far-fetched.* I emailed my proposals to Dawn The Younger, and in the subject line, typed the words, "I failed."

She, however, called my offerings brilliant and crowned me the Title Queen. It's doubtful she's right about that.

In the center of the museum, The Obvious. Note the

angelic harp music as you pass under the arched entryway. Here we display only two lovelies, the foundation of the collection.

First, sitting on an ebony pedestal: *I am African American*. Notice how the light dances off... oh dear, the staff neglected to return Black History Month to storage. Please be aware of sharp edges as you walk past: *Here we go again, the same old documentary about the Edmund Pettis Bridge*.

Next to it, a companion piece, equally hallowed, multi-faceted, glowing pink: *I'm a woman*. Its curves complement the angularity of *African American*. These masterpieces set the tone for everything else in the collection.

Push on a heart-shaped brick. Voila. The wall gives way to a secret passage—The Tunnel of Family Heirlooms. Keep moving. Otherwise, tentacles will wrap around your ankles and snatch you off your feet. *You can't afford, you can't afford, you can't afford:* a broken record bequeathed to me from Dad. From Mother (or stepmother, technically—she married Dad when I was twelve): *You're too pretty to wear beige all the time* and *Wash the dishes, dammit*.

The sealed chest in the corner? My biological mother dropped it off. Didn't get a chance to sort through it before she died. Suspect I'll need a therapist to break the lock.

Although the title of boss belongs to me, my control is tenuous. Pieces go missing. The last time a subscription form demanded a phone number, the once-familiar digits evaporated. The route to my favorite thrift store disappeared. Along with the name of the actress who starred in that HBO movie last month.

On the other hand, I've been trying since 1972 to get rid of the theme song from *The Beverly Hillbillies*.

The museum also houses artifacts of unknown origin. While cleaning the kitchen, I worried about Marissa, who'd asked for advice about her current romance. Why did she date such inappropriate men? Midway through scouring the sink, it occurred to me I didn't know anybody named Marissa.

On the third day of a weeklong meditation retreat, panic startled me awake. I'd forgotten to supply the neighbors with my dog's medicine. Retreat rules dictated we refrain from speaking, except in case of emergency. Would canine healthcare fall under that guideline? I steeled myself to discuss my plight with the teacher and then make the phone call that would save my pooch, but stopped short in the hallway. I didn't own a dog.

Despite significant investment in security, danger threatens. Here in tornado alley, a single twister could wipe out my entire collection, sending regrets and intentions flying across the plains, to land on an unsuspecting grandma in Topeka, who isn't the least bit interested—because she collects spoons.

Or worse, a Buddhist sutra might illuminate the place, exposing plaster façades masquerading as granite, linoleum floors passing for marble. It's rumored that thunderclaps of revelation wreak havoc with one's cogitation. Beliefs, mistaken for diamonds, could shatter like glass. Doubts might crumble. Fantasies explode. And in the rubble, the purpose of my mind revealed: it stores dusty souvenirs from a not-so-unique life.

Anyhoo, just a thought.

The Price:
Desire is More than I Bargained For

My reflection in the closet mirror came very close to pleasing me. Bootcut slacks balanced the hips, just as the ad promised. A cardigan skimmed over my torso, completing the hoped-for slenderizing line from shoulders to shoes. Very flattering, just about perfect, but missing something.

Ahh. A yellow purse.

I thought it was only a passing fancy.

Forgot about the purse as soon as I closed the closet door, but it tempted me in the evening, when well-dressed actresses sashayed through television commercials. It seduced me from the pages of mail-order catalogs. It flirted with me as I waited for a table at a restaurant. In January, I thought a yellow purse would look cute with my jeans. By March I was sure it would transform me into a better person.

I can't live another day without a yellow purse.

I stalked department stores, on the hunt for the lifesaving handbag. Tote bags, wallets, and clutches covered the shelves. But no. It had to be a shoulder bag. Shoulder bags abounded—in shades of mustard, lemon, and gold. But no. It had to be daffodil. The repeated failures did not discourage me. They intensified my greed.

The ache of desire was familiar. It started in the morning shower. I disdained the bar of soap, didn't care that it was scented with lavender, handcrafted by local artisans, and beneficial to the environment. Body wash would be better. When thirst sent me to the refrigerator, I pushed aside the orange juice, diet pop, and bottled water. *Where's the iced tea?* Evening ended with a final foot wiggle in the search for a more comfortable sleeping position.

The pocketbook quest remained a solo mission (girlfriends would taint it with their own ideas about handbag lust) until I told the secret to my trendy sister.

Leslie plopped down beside me on her bed. "Something's wrong. I can tell."

"I've been looking for a yellow purse," I said. "Can't find one that will work."

She opened a dresser drawer. "Really? How about this? Brand new, and you can have it." She pulled out a box that emitted a faint glow. She parted the tissue paper. There lay a zippered pouf made of leather that shone like a jonquil in the midday sun. It was the size of a lunchbox, with inside pockets for keys, phone, and glasses.

I was overjoyed. The thirst finally quenched.

I sucked in my breath. "Why are you giving it away?"

Surely this prize came with a price.

"You know me. Always grabbing things on sale. It's been sitting here for months."

She found my old purse and switched the contents to its replacement. "Besides, it's cuter than this granny thing you carry."

I slung the bag onto my shoulder and headed for the

bathroom mirror. The pop of color peeked from under my sweater's gray sleeve. Leather nestled against ribcage, a fit as familiar as the embrace of a long-lost friend.

I turned away from my reflection only long enough to kiss Leslie on the cheek. "Thank you. It's perfect."

The daffodil pouf collected compliments on its first outing. The teenaged girl who rang up my groceries stopped to marvel. "Oh-my-god. I love your purse."

A colleague I admired for her elegance caught up with me after a meeting. "Beautiful bag."

An artist friend snatched it off my arm. "That color. Fabulous."

On days when I dressed up, the bag put the period at the end of my carefully constructed fashion statement. And if I threw on dirty jeans and tucked my hair under a baseball cap, the purse evoked mystery. *Is she really a frumpy hausfrau or a movie star in disguise?*

My confidence brightened.

I sent Leslie a thank-you card, which gushed over her generosity and recounted the exploits of the handbag. She phoned me to acknowledge the card. Her gift had improved our relationship as well as my image. Life settled into quiet perfection.

Until a worn spot erupted on the strap.

I panicked. I could not let the bag wear out. Fate had brought us together.

There was only one recourse. Save it for special occasions, and buy an additional purse for every day. I would have my daffodil cake and eat it, too.

I put away the favored bag after dumping its contents back into the one it had replaced. With a satisfying slam of the closet door, I took off on a new mission.

Greed propelled me into a high-tech search. Each

morning, I rolled out of bed and stumbled straight to the laptop. Google returned 37,000,000 results for the query *yellow handbag*. Photos the size of postage stamps wallpapered the screen. Pop-up ads tempted me. Blogs about shopping led to YouTube videos showing women unboxing designer bags, luring me ever deeper into the Internet. While others checked stock tickers, I was glued to the falling prices on purses.

Late afternoons, the room grew murky as dusk settled. Gnawing at my temples intensified, because I was subsisting on protein bars and energy drinks. Knots tightened my belly, but like indigestion after Thanksgiving gluttony, they were a small price to pay.

On the third day of the fourth week, I pried myself away from the computer, determined to exchange my jammies for jeans. With the closet door half-open, I squinted into the shadows.

The daffodil pouf gleamed back. The ultimate yellow bag. The preeminent pocketbook. The Holy Grail of handbags. Exactly what I was looking for.

I felt betrayed. It turned out that green grass was plentiful on my side of the fence. I was doomed. If owning the treasures I coveted failed to gratify me, I might never be happy. The future looked grim—a closet bursting with the spoils of my acquisitiveness, shelves crashing to the floor under the weight of the loot, and ambulance drivers pulling my squashed body from beneath a mountain of cashmere, silk, and suede. Death from insatiable accessorizing.

Yet hope rose from my pile of luxuries. After all, I'd been content with the "granny thing," right up until the instant the cute-yellow-bag passing fancy had failed to pass. It wasn't the *lack* of a new purse that felt bad; it was the *wanting* that made me sick. Even then, the sickness only showed up in fits and starts. Maybe... if I caught desire before *it* caught *me*...

I set the pouf beside its drab companion. Once more, the transfer began. I tossed in the wallet. Keys, phone, and glasses slid into the pockets. That worn spot seemed smaller.

I felt calmer, if somewhat weary from the journey. A hot shower beckoned me. Pulsing water pounded out the tension. Steam eased away the kinks. The fragrance of lavender wafted up from the eco-friendly bar of soap. *Hmm. Wouldn't some body wash be nice?*

Time held its breath, but I allowed the question to dissolve into the mist. The price of responding was too high.

Freeways, Foothills, and Phobias:
Courage Takes a Sunday Drive

Alone and lost, I snaked uphill on a two-lane road in the foothills. Anger disrupted my concentration. The intended plan for this final day of my California vacation? Me in the passenger seat, sipping a cold pop and soaking up the scenery. My brother was supposed to be driving. That didn't pan out.

Brother Dear had gone off on his own escapade, instead of chauffeuring me to the Hindu temple for which I currently searched. He'd sent me off with written directions and a cheery, "Have a good time."

His instructions had culminated in a "soft Y intersection," whatever the heck that was. Hoping to coax it into existence, I leaned forward against the steering wheel and squinted at the sun. The horizon receded. Street signs materialized, raised my hopes, dashed them, slid past. As each one disappeared, my palms grew clammier and my mouth drier.

Vacations. I was secretly afraid of them. The mere thought of them made me tremble like an acrophobic facing a ladder. Every holiday became an exercise in avoiding risk while maintaining an illusion of carefree abandon. It was necessary to frequent the same haunts year after year and create meticulous plans, in order to avoid spontaneity. Whenever it threatened, I reneged on commitments, turned down invitations, and passed up adventures. My mantra was *no thanks, think I'll stay in and read.*

The shrinking of my world came into focus after eighty-year-old Uncle Al returned from an Alaskan cruise. He lamented it was his last, because he'd sailed to every destination offered by every cruise line. Twenty years his junior, lacking the courage to venture to foreign ports, passport used only for airport identification, I was sick of being a chicken.

A visit halfway across the country presented the opportunity to force a showdown with my tendency to cower under the covers. First, I confronted the quaking woman in the bathroom mirror. *Listen up, scaredy cat. You're not the boss of me anymore.* Next, grabbed my favorite blankey. Finally, flopped onto the bed and opened the laptop.

According to the airlines, a circuitous route cost a hundred dollars less than a direct flight to my destination, Santa Barbara. That meant landing in Los Angeles and then driving up the coast. The cursor blinked over the purchase icon. Drive through big city traffic? My car shaking in the wake of more confident vehicles, horns nagging from behind at every stoplight? I bought the more expensive flight, straight into Santa Barbara.

My sister Leslie met me at the airport, escorted me to the car rental booth, and lobbied for an upgrade. "You always go for the dinky, cheap cars. Try something new."

Something new. My cheeks heated up. I was terrified to operate a full-sized sedan, but embarrassed to look bad by saying no. I nodded to the clerk, and she handed over the keys to a Toyota Camry.

Fortunately, Leslie insisted on driving. She eased the car out of the parking lot. She played the dashboard like a baby grand. "Where's my station? Let's crank up the AC." She poked and prodded the new toy. I was afraid to break it.

The next day I phoned my best friend, who lived in Los Angeles. According to my plan, she would motor up to Santa Barbara for our reunion. Instead, she asked that we meet at a restaurant midway between the two cities. "Girlfriend, you know I love you, but I do *not* feel like driving."

Neither did I, but she'd made the trip many times. I would have to drive through the big city after all. What with urban sprawl, the midpoint lay well inside Los Angeles.

On the agreed-upon day, I washed down a couple of aspirins with a few gulps of antacid and pointed the car toward LA.

The highway paralleled the ocean. Nothing chased away my demons like the Southern California coastline on a cloudless morning. A press of the window button sucked a rush of salt-scented air into the car. The Pacific sprayed mist against my face. Gulls screamed. Wind whipped through my hair.

The road turned inland, and I shivered. Straight ahead lay the Conejo Grade, a three-mile 1,000-foot rise in elevation.

Back in the 1970s—my apartment in LA and my family in Santa Barbara—I'd been a regular commuter on the Conejo Grade. In the '70s, the grade tormented my no-frills used car. The little coupe, its plugs rusted and engine in need of a tune-up, strained all the way. The temperature needle crept toward the red. Every time my rolling wreck finally crested the summit, its cruising speed had dropped from sixty-five to ten. But that was in the 1970s.

Forty years later—brand new sedan. The speed remained constant, the temperature gauge stock-still.

Forty years later—same old sissy. Palms still sweaty,

stomach still queasy. I fought with the past for every yard of progress up the hill, resisting the urge to drift into the slow lane... to let up on the accelerator... to throw up.

I exited the highway, pulled over, and studied the directions scribbled on a fast-food receipt. Left, right, left, left. Landmarks appeared on cue. Tension settled down to a manageable level, until a traffic sign appeared that read, "Not a Through Street." Anxiety returned. Self-criticism followed. After all, it was a sun-washed morning in California, not a freezing night on Everest. It was a road sign, for God's sake, not a nascent avalanche. But there I sat, temples pulsing, shoulders aching, bravado cringing under the seat.

The street ended in a turn-around landscaped with roses in full bloom. Half a bottle of Pepto-Bismol later, the restaurant parking lot came into view.

My buddy greeted me with open arms. "Girl, you look fantastic. So happy and calm. What's your secret?"

Decades of practice made me proficient at being a fraud.

The trip to LA produced a migraine that validated my distaste for exploring what other people called scenic byways. I preferred the predictable grid created by north-south intersecting east-west, unless I occupied the passenger seat while someone else took the wheel.

That was the intention for the final day of vacation. Wayne and I planned to visit a Hindu temple in the Santa Ynez Mountains. He volunteered to drive. The trip would be a tonic: a time to relax, enjoy the view, and give up the quest for bravery.

When he announced his plans had changed, I felt like a five-year-old, all dressed up for a birthday party that had just been canceled.

He offered an alternative. "It's easy to find. You can still go by yourself."

"No thanks. Think I'll... well... okay."

He proceeded, pre-GPS. "At the last Santa Barbara exit, turn left under the bridge. Drive the frontage road to the deer trail that follows the ridgeline, and then snake around the switchbacks until you come to a soft Y intersection. The sign for the temple is painted on a rock."

I punched him on the shoulder.

"On second thought, I'll MapQuest it for you," he said.

The two sets of directions bore no common traits, except the left turn from the exit. A toddler could have figured that out. A right turn off the interstate plunged one into the Pacific.

Lost after ten minutes, I stopped for directions at a grocery store, where the clerk explained that the route was simpler than it sounded. But longer.

I clutched the wheel, praying for that soft Y turn. Million-dollar homes peeked from among the pines. The trip meter turned over every tenth mile with the persistence of a dripping faucet. My head was pounding, squeezed between a longing for immediate rescue and an intolerance for foolish overreaction.

I pulled into a driveway to allow a train of cars to go around. Flashes of color bobbed in the side mirror. Balloons attached to a mailbox indicated a realtor's open house. The display marked a subtle curve in the road, where a lane hardly wider than the driveway intersected my route. The elusive soft Y turn.

Woohoo! The lane led straight to the rock that marked the entrance to the temple grounds.

Safe in the parking lot, I rested my head on the steering wheel and bit my bottom lip to keep it from trembling. It trembled anyway.

My big showdown backfired. Instead of helping me to

overcome my fears, this stupid vacation had invited them along to taunt me. New-car nervousness. City-driving anxiety. Altered-plan phobia. Fancy words for chicken.

An urge to cry surprised and embarrassed me.

Grabbing the keys, I shoved open the door and stumbled out of the car.

The lot was deserted. Thank goodness I could pull myself together without any onlookers. I leaned against the car frame with my arms on the roof. I'd made it this far, may as well have a look around.

Evergreen shrubs surrounded the parking area. Beyond them, pines. Mountain peaks—blue-gray specters in the distance—soared over the treetops.

Made it.

A breeze carried the scent of eucalyptus.

Me.

The scaredy cat had ascended the Conejo Grade. The homebody had forged past the dead-end sign. The bookworm had climbed through the foothills.

Me.

Who'd put down her novel, changed her plans, and tackled an adventure. I'll be damned. I made it.

A deep breath puffed up my chest and a sigh released my past. I slammed the car door closed.

A footpath wound uphill, but no building was visible from the parking lot. A familiar ache crept across my brow. After all this, still no temple. I reached for the door handle.

Wait a minute... maybe the building's around that bend. Yeah.

I tossed the keys into the air, caught them in one hand, and strode up the path.

Attachments:
I Can't Let Go, Despite the Wisdom of Nonattachment

The Apron

Mama's eyes were green. That's what everybody says. Green eyes that speckled gold in a certain light. Her hair fell in black waves below her shoulders. At home, she often wore a short-sleeved housedress—a shapeless drift of faded stripes—and pink slippers with a band of fluff across each instep.

Saturdays when I was ten, she cooked up chili for supper. She slipped a bib apron over her head. The waist strings looped into a bow behind her, and a strap fastened across her shoulder blades with two white buttons.

On chili nights, I perched on a red Formica step stool near the kitchen table. Did she feel my eyes on her, sense a warm spot on her back just beneath those buttons?

We lived in Des Moines when Mama cooked chili, but I was born in Ottumwa. According to family legend, she was playing gin rummy with friends when labor pains began. Dad chuckled whenever he repeated the story. "Catherine was beating the pants off us. She hated to leave for the hospital." Mama enjoyed a good time. Or... she considered the baby in her belly an inconvenience. You can spin it either way.

In my earliest Ottumwa memory, my brother Bill and I—both of us toddlers—are jumping on a couch, trampoline-style. Stuffing erupts from the seams with every impact. I'm wearing underpants; Bill's in a diaper. Mama's a ghost in the background. Not rushing toward us, arms outstretched. Not warning us to stop tearing up the furniture. Not worrying we'd fall and crack our heads.

We lived in a shotgun house. A living room in the front, where eight-year-old twins Michael and Michelle slept. Behind that, a bedroom with a king bed for Dad and Mama and bunk beds shoved against a wall for Bill and me. Behind that, the kitchen, which led into a shed Dad added on to the rear of the house. You had to walk through the shed, crammed with tools and fishing tackle, to get to the back yard.

Someone once took a picture of Mama and me, posed side-by-side in the outside doorway of the shed. The black interior pressed against us from behind, filled in the space between our rigid bodies. Mama's arms were folded across her chest. Her expression was opaque, attention drawn to something that excluded me. Maybe sheets hanging limp on the clothesline that stretched between the shed and the outhouse. Maybe a sudden movement in the pen where Dad's coon hounds dozed.

Shortly after that picture was taken, we moved to Des Moines, into a two-story house. A staircase ascended from the living room. Midway to the second floor, it took a hard left turn at a landing, then climbed to a hallway that connected three bedrooms and a bath. The landing made a cozy reading nook—a beam of light streamed in through a little window. Sometimes my siblings and I crouched on the top step, straining toward the muffled angry voices behind our parents' door. We huddled together, but independent, no gestures of comfort offered to one another. With my fingertip, I drew circles in the dust that covered the wood floor.

On the nights Mama cooked up chili, she scuffed around the kitchen, icebox to cabinet to stove. Pink slippers stark against linoleum grayed from ground-in footprints. She leaned over a skillet, hand on hip, stirring, while hamburger hissed and crackled. Steam moistened the air. She stopped to lift the hair away from the nape of her neck. Did she feel my eyes on her, where baby hairs lay fine and straight against her skin?

My parents divorced when I was twelve. Dad married Kim Carol, who became my new mother. They decided to move the family out to California. On the day we left in our caravan of three cars and a U-Haul, I wonder... did Mama wave goodbye from our front porch? Did she pat away a tear with the hem of her apron?

Mama's eyes were green. That's what everybody says. On Saturday nights, before she started on the chili, she tossed a dishtowel over one shoulder and then tied an apron behind her. Did she feel my gaze on her hand, just where the wedding band glinted as her fingers worked the strings into a bow? Maybe she didn't know I was perched on a step stool an arm's length away. Every Saturday night.

If only I'd tugged her apron strings, she might have turned her face toward mine... and possibly, I'd know today that Mama's eyes were green.

Bingo

On weekends I escaped my freshman year by skulking back to my parents' house—a place just as hateful as college. Dad and Mother Kim always wanted to talk, which was a euphemism for their blend of interrogation and unsolicited advice. I just wanted to light a stick of incense and curl up under my covers. On campus, I shied away from the unrestricted access to booze, sex, and parties. As much as I'd railed against my high school curfew, it had given me cover. So on weekends during my freshman year, I dragged myself home on the Greyhound. There was nowhere else to go.

Mother Kim picked me up from the bus station. She chipped away at my stoicism with questions about classes. undeterred by monosyllables mumbled in response. At home, I followed her through the front door and down our shadowed hallway to my room.

The suitcase thudded onto the floor.

She swept her hand across the closet shelf. "I cleaned out the closets and gave away that stuffed dog. You didn't want it, did you?"

She gave away Bingo?

My head felt heavy as I raised my gaze to the spot my stuffed pooch used to occupy. A lump in my throat prevented me from speaking. Besides, it was too late. Bingo was gone.

"You didn't want it, did you?"

"Uh . . . guess not."

Bingo was gone.

My grandmother, Mon, had given me the Dalmatian for Christmas. She named him Bingo. His ears flopped, but his body was stiff. He was permanently posed in a standing position, ready for duty at the front of a fire engine. Feet planted. Tail pointing straight out behind him. Chin up. Black plastic nose. Glass eyes. A red ribbon tied in a bow around his neck. Alert for the first sign of a little girl who needed to be rescued.

The morning after Christmas, I was sitting at the table with Mon. We were the slowest eaters in the family, so we had the kitchen to ourselves.

She pushed her plate aside and picked up Bingo, who was standing guard beside my chair. She laid him in her lap and tapped out a tune on his side. A bell inside his ear jingled as she sang. "B-I-N-G-O. B-I-N-G-O. B-I-N-G-O. And Bingo was his name-oh."

Mon and Bingo and me. When you have two brothers and a sister and you're the quiet one who plays alone on the landing so nobody will tease you, and there's only one grandmother to go around... Mon and Bingo and me. My longing stretched the memory like taffy.

All through grade school, after bedtime, the television downstairs blared creepy music from *The Outer Limits* and *Twilight Zone*. I was alone, the room was pitch-black, and another nightmare was on the way. Bingo snuggled under the covers with me, my arm hooked around his middle. I sang just loud enough to drown out Rod Serling, but not loud enough to tip off my location to the monsters. "B-I-N-G-O. B-I-N-G-O. B-I-N-G-O. And Bingo was his name-oh."

Bingo guarded my dresser all through junior high and then moved to the closet floor, somewhere among the dirty clothes. He stayed there during my high school years. And I was probably too embarrassed to take him to college, but I knew exactly where to find him in case of an emergency.

Until Mother Kim cleaned the closet.

Bingo didn't cross my mind for thirty years, until I began composing an essay about Mother Kim. A treatise filled with the insights of a fifty-year-old. At a critical juncture in my analysis, my fingers stopped typing of their own accord. The screen pulsed iridescent light into the room.

"You gave away Bingo?" I screamed. "He wasn't some... toy." I threw a pencil at the wall. "He was mine, not yours."

I snapped the laptop shut and paced around the house. How could she do that? The refrigerator offered no solace. Why couldn't I stand up to her? A kick of the trashcan sent papers flying but did not improve my mood. How could she die before I told her off? I stomped upstairs, flung myself on the bed and pulled the covers over my head.

Bingo was gone.

I didn't even get to say goodbye.

Kwan Yin

When I was in my thirties, Mother Kim tended her roses in a sunny corner of my parents' California backyard, otherwise shaded by diminutive fruit trees. They bore apples and oranges and enough avocados to keep the neighborhood swimming in guacamole. Mother placed a statue of Kwan Yin, goddess of compassion, beneath one of the orange trees. Serenity rendered in concrete.

A pathway led from the front of my parents' house to the back, along the side of the attached garage. Crimson bougainvillea arched over the path and lay across the roof. With the sun at the right angle, the narrow passage looked like a shimmering entry to Eden.

Inside, the house was gloomy. Only one burner on the stove worked. After the dishwasher broke, Mother stored boxes of cereal in it.

Summers, I visited to help out with chores they were too old to perform. Mother slept alone in their king-sized bed, while Dad slept on a twin in the garage apartment, its one window shadowed by the bougainvillea.

"Do you and Dad ever get together?" I asked Mother.

"Only when you kids come home."

I reacted like a self-absorbed teenager, realizing my parents had essentially split up. They'd betrayed me. How long had this been going on? Why hadn't I been informed? Theirs was a solid marriage; they appeared to be passionately in love. Relationships look different from the inside than from the outside, and I was learning I had been on the outside of this one.

Dad, to me. "Climb up on a ladder and trim that goddamned vine. It's growing under the shingles."

Mother. "Don't you dare cut down my bougainvillea."

Me. "But Dad said—."

I escaped to commiserate with Kwan Yin. *When did my father start cussing like that?*

Back when I was in high school, my parents were Beautiful People. Natalie Wood and Sidney Poitier. They gave parties, which I suspect my mother fancied as literary salons. There was champagne, wall-to-wall books. Dad wrote a column for three newspapers and taught creative writing. Mother was a poet. Their friends—writers, artists, old hippies, and spiritual seekers—orbited around them.

I told Kwan Yin my parents had been happy then. Kwan Yin said nothing.

I walked in the front door and found them sitting in the shadows in the living room.

Mother, to me. "Your father's having an affair."

Dad. "What about you? Sleeping with that man ten years ago?"

Mother. "That was different. We agreed to an open marriage then."

Me. "What—?"

I returned the summer after that.

Mother, to me. "Give me a ride to the store. Your father won't take me."

Dad, to me. "You always follow your mother around. Pay attention to me sometime."

I was embarrassed and surprised. All the famous people Dad knew, and he wanted to spend time with me?

Me. "But Mother wanted—"

I asked Kwan Yin if the smartest people in the world ended up like this, what chance at happiness did I have? She wouldn't say.

It was spring the last time I went home, after Mother was diagnosed with cancer, after her mastectomy and radiation. She moaned in her sleep in her bedroom. Dad, sick with lung disease, coughed in his garage. To let sun into his apartment, I trimmed the bougainvillea. Its thorns drew blood. On days I was too weary to speak, Kwan Yin listened anyway.

After Mother died, Kwan Yin reigned over my backyard. I plucked dandelions from around my rose bushes, and Kwan Yin listened to my proof that my parents had been happy: They wrote a book together. They took care of Dad's aging mother together. They went to church together. They had all those charming friends.

As I passed middle age, I yielded to an urge to simplify. I cleaned out closets, rid myself of clothes and memories that no longer fit. I gave Kwan Yin to a friend who'd turned her backyard into a meditation garden.

But I can't help thinking, if we'd had a few more days together, I'd have convinced Kwan Yin that my parents—the smartest people in the world—had been happy once.

The Fleet

"You driving that stupid car again?" My sister Leslie snatched a wad of lint from my curls, threw it on the ground, and stomped on it. She patted my hair back into place. "Look what he's doing to you."

Summers—after I'd married and moved away—I flew back home to visit my siblings and help my aging parents with chores and errands. Like my father, I was too cheap to rent transportation. Besides, Dad owned a fleet.

The Stupid Car. Wayne had bought the '75 Oldsmobile his freshman year of college for $900. When he upgraded in 1991, he gave it to Dad, a gift accepted without a thank you. My brother's departure for school left Dad as the only one to chauffeur Mother to the grocery store. The chore became one of his many resentments, barnacles attached to his bent and shrinking frame.

The Stupid Car was a faded robin's-egg blue with rusted chrome. The passenger side mirror dangled like a broken wing. Dad plastered parking permits—from the college where he taught creative writing—across the windshield, leaving one unobstructed corner above the steering wheel. The torn headliner draped from the ceiling and grazed the head of whoever was driving. It bled white fluff.

The Camper. A 1964 Corvair pickup with a camper on the bed. Whenever my five siblings and I gathered at the family house for the holidays, Mother wanted to transport us to Sunday service at the Vedanta Temple, where she and Dad were regular parishioners. My sister and brother owned cars of their own, but neither wanted to attempt following Dad in a caravan. Dad's solution: "We'll take the camper. Put the kids in the back."

The back of The Camper enclosed six cubic feet of space.

Two horizontal surfaces passed for seating—no windows. We stuffed ourselves inside like so much lumber. Clutched the stove or the edge of the table or somebody's leg, as Dad careened through the California foothills. When we arrived at the temple, we spilled out, bruised and seasick.

The Truck. An '89 Ford crew cab dually with an extended bed. Dad cursed the birds when they pooped on it, but he refused to buy a car cover. "Waste of money." He rarely drove the Ford, because it only got sixteen miles to the gallon.

He laid down one rule. "Don't let me catch you in my truck."

So I drove The Stupid Car.

Dad and Mother became foster parents to their four-year-old great grandson, Anthony. It fell to me to get Anthony to and from pre-school, but one Friday when it was time to pick him up, The Stupid Car was missing. Dad must have forgotten the schedule. I waited, paced, checked my watch.

Screw it. I grabbed the keys to The Truck. How could he possibly punish a grown woman? And why was a grown woman afraid of getting into trouble anyway?

As soon as I stepped up into the cab and backed into the street, I fell in love. No wonder Dad wanted to keep it for himself. The Truck towered over every car on the road between home and daycare. Only five feet three, I felt avenged for every movie I'd suffered through with my view blocked by a six-footer.

I parked at the school and fetched Anthony from his classroom. When he saw The Truck, he shook his head. "Grandpa's gonna kill you."

We pulled into the drive. Dad was standing in the front doorway. "You little bitch. You took my truck."

Oh my god. Dad just called me a bitch.

I felt the urge to duck, but the toxin in his words immobilized me. "I had to get Anthony."

How could he call me a bitch?

Anthony's hand slid out of mine, as he skirted around Dad into the house. My father's eyes narrowed to slits. His jaw moved sideways as his tongue worked his dentures. "Told you not to take my truck." He turned away, slinking into the shadows of the living room.

I went numb, smothered my hurt like it was a grease fire.

Dad died a year later, and The Fleet was sold off. If only I could visit one last time... puffed up with my writing success. I'd pull up in a rented luxury sedan, strut past The Camper, The Stupid Car, and The Truck. I'd march right up to Dad, hands on my hips.

"Listen, old man. You can keep your junkyard clunkers. I rented a brand new Beemer. You know what else? I... am... not ... a... bitch. I'm your little girl."

Mirror, Mirror:
What, Me Prejudiced?

"This must have been written by some illiterate Italian who can't speak English." The remark slid off the pastor's tongue as he read the announcements from the church bulletin. He chuckled about the typos he was encountering, but he did not smile.

I gasped, then elbowed my husband. "Did you hear that? He just made a racist joke."

Ben's words came slowly. "I know... yeah..." He seemed alarmed, but not as mad as I was.

We had visited the church on a whim the previous Sunday, having just moved into a house down the street. We returned, because Ben liked the music. I was wary. It appeared I was the only black person in the congregation.

The preacher's insult outraged me. I took it personally. If he joked like that about Italians, Lord knows what he'd say about *me*.

I inventoried the possibilities. In my twenties, hard at work as the front desk clerk of a resort hotel: a guest sneered that my kind were fit only to clean rooms. In my thirties, driving my mother to the store: a pedestrian screamed a racial epithet at me and added an obscene gesture. In my forties, paused at a stoplight in the suburbs: the driver of a pick-up pulled up in the next lane, rolled down his window, and spat the *N* word. The preacher had said "illiterate Italian," but I heard a lifetime of *nigger*.

It scared me, too. If a minister was prejudiced, I couldn't trust anyone. I longed to give him the benefit of the doubt. Longed for the other parishioners to validate my indignation, to stand up and demand an apology. But people sitting nearby made no sounds or gestures I could interpret as protest. Maybe they agreed with the slur. Maybe they wanted me out of their church. Maybe they hated me. It was no longer Kansas City, 2003. It was Montgomery, 1961.

I was desperate to leave but couldn't move. Wanted to disappear, but could only stare into the distance. Just as I had at sixteen, when my white stepmother took me to see *Gone with the Wind*. I hated Mammy's black face, shining like polished leather under that stupid bandana. I hated Prissy's simpering uselessness, hated her for being exactly what Rhett Butler called her. A "simple-minded darkie." After the matinee, my stepmom and I edged through a crowd of movie-goers who looked like her—fair skin, straight hair, thin lips. I was Prissy.

The pastor moved on to his sermon, but the pounding in my chest drowned out the message. In fact, I composed a lecture of my own, filled with *how-dare-yous* and *shame-on-yous* and a fusillade of *you-don't-knows*.

Stripped of the option to fight, run, or vanish, I struggled to find calm within a torrent of passions. As Ben cradled my hand in his, my agitation collapsed under its own weight, exposing a grief that rendered me as useless as Prissy.

After the service, I said, "I'm going down to meet the minister."

Ben chuckled. "Right. I'll bet you are."

He was wrong if he suspected an argument between his

wife and the unsuspecting preacher. My expression might have signaled confidence, but I was trembling. Words were too limiting to encapsulate the complicated feelings that lay beneath my initial indignation.

The pastor stood at the front of the church, greeting parishioners. I trudged down the aisle toward him. He smiled when we shook hands.

I pushed my dreadlocks off my face and took a deep breath. "We... my husband and I... visited last Sunday... and today. We felt welcome... until that joke about Italians. I don't feel welcome anymore."

His smile dissolved.

"Oh. Let me explain. We're doing a pizza fundraiser with an Italian restaurant and—"

"I'm not here to accuse you of anything. Or make assumptions about your motives." Maybe there was still a way to let him off the hook, to end this awkward exchange. Usually the one who shrank away from conflict, this time—surprising myself as well as the preacher—I stood firm. "That remark... it made me think... when will it be my turn? When will you all make fun of me?"

"That won't ever happen. When you get to know me better, you'll understand."

He touted his accomplishments in the area of diversity. He listed the church's contributions to civic committees, initiatives on behalf of immigrants, and programs for inner city youth. It sounded like he was giving a presentation to the Chamber of Commerce.

I waited for him to finish. "I'm new to your church. Didn't know you when you made the joke."

Neither of us budged, until he let out a long breath. "I apologize. It wasn't very smart. Thank you for your courage... and honesty." He draped his arm across my shoulders, uninvited. "I hope you and your husband will come back."

I cringed, took a step backward, then turned away to search for Ben.

We walked to the car in silence. He eased it out of the parking lot into the street. "Awfully quiet. You okay?"

"No."

"What happened?"

"Well, he's not a bad guy. But good people are worse."

"Meaning?"

"They're so sure about not being prejudiced. They don't listen. They just brag about—"

"What?"

I smacked the dashboard. "No. I don't believe it."

Months earlier, at my nephew's football game, I crossed an urban high school campus in search of other team parents. I felt out of place, probably the only black person there who'd be rooting for the suburban Catholic school my nephew attended. Three African-American teenagers sauntered toward me, dressed in baggy pants and shirts that hung to their knees. Shoulder punching emphasized the boys' banter, laced with an occasional "Dude" and "Bro." Their joking grew louder as they approached.

I stopped them when they got close. "Is the football field in this direction?"

"Yes, ma'am. If you continue down the walkway, you'll find it directly on your left," one of them said.

And then all three in unison. "Have a nice day."

Their response caught me off guard, but I didn't know why. I dismissed it and hurried off, intent on my destination. The unnamed irritant stopped me midstride. I turned around. The young men continued on their way. Their voices faded into the autumn breeze.

As they vanished around a corner, the truth about my discomfort hit me.

I'd expected those black teenagers to talk like gangster rappers, but they'd addressed me in tones as courtly as those of British noblemen.

By the time I finished telling Ben my story, we'd arrived home and pulled into our garage. I glanced over at him, sheepish, then quickly looked away. Maybe we'd come to the same conclusion. If he said it first, it would spare me from admitting it out loud. Instead, he reached across the console and patted my knee. Sitting in the car, surrounded by everything familiar and safe, I was undone. Hoping to escape the moment, I gazed out my window. My reflection stared back, as my thoughts returned to the church.

When I'd faced that minister, I'd looked straight into a mirror.

Part II

Bad Things Happen to Good People—If They're Lucky:
Transcending Difficulties

A thunderstorm slowed traffic to a crawl. Through the rain pelting my windshield, I could make out only a string of blinking brake lights. The eighteen-wheeler in the next lane was about to squash me from the right side, and you could have surfed on the wave thrown up by the cocky four-by-four passing on my left. I white-knuckled the steering wheel and prayed for a miracle to get myself home. Alone on the highway. My fate looked bleak.

Actually, it was a good day to die.

I was in love.

The house was clean.

Alone in the Dark:
Meditating at a War-Torn Peace Rally

"Excuse me, lady."

At first, the words meant nothing to me, feeble competition for midday sun that eased the chill from autumn and brightened the colorful activity at my feet. I was strolling among the chalk drawings of La Estrada Dell'Arte, a sidewalk art show. Unable to draw worth a hoot, I was in awe of what others could do with chalk.

Local Picassos knelt on the concrete in front of Kansas City's Union Station to sketch landscapes, abstracts, or still-lifes. One artist hunched over his masterpiece as if in prayer, while Coltrane offered up a hymn from a CD player. A group of teenagers collaborated as they munched snacks and tossed wisecracks. I had just stepped around a reproduction of one of Warhol's *Campbell's Soup Cans* (tomato) and was admiring a six-foot portrait of Madonna, when the voice broke into my consciousness.

"Excuse me. In the red *sweater.*" A Gen X'er with tousled brown hair waved in my direction and hurried to catch up with me. Grinning, he closed the gap between us. He wore the expression of a twelve-year-old boy surprised to find himself face-to-face with his favorite major-league pitcher.

"My name's Randy. You're going to think this is crazy, but I'm painting your portrait."

The introduction was so outrageous and the young man's demeanor so unthreatening, all I could do was chuckle. His wide-eyed innocence disarmed me. His excitement was infectious. I *wanted* to talk to this Randy person. How in the heck would he follow up that opening?

We shook hands. "I'm Dawn. You're painting me?"

He shifted his weight from one foot to the other and back again. "Yeah. I'm sure it's you. I'm pretty sure. Were you at the war protest last year on the Plaza?" he asked.

"Yes."

"Were you sitting on a blanket with three other women?"

"Yes."

His words tumbled out like clothes from a dryer opened mid-cycle. "I knew it... I recognize your dreadlocks... what were you thinking when you did that... I know what it means to me... you were so courageous."

The protest he referred to had occurred just prior to the 2003 US invasion of Iraq. Peace activists had organized weekend rallies in a midtown park. Randy had shown his support for peace by attending one of the rallies. My friends and I had shown ours by meditating in the middle of the demonstrators. He saw us there and then reproduced the scene in watercolor.

I hesitated when I approached the scene that first Sunday, an afternoon in early spring when winter cold still bit. I stepped onto the grass and gasped, panic-stricken, at the edge of the park. Many who *supported* the invasion had shown up to protest the protest. Groups with disparate views stood on the curb, their hand-lettered signs held high. They confronted each other and the drivers of passing cars, with shouts of "Support our troops" or "Stay out of Iraq." Inside the park, a circle of drummers kept up an incessant beat. A teenager danced alone, accompanied by rap music on his boom box. Community leaders crowded onto a platform in front of a microphone. Each in turn screamed red-faced opposition to the war. In the middle of this commotion, people walked their dogs, which added nervous yelping to the mix.

I don't like crowds.

I don't like dogs.

I don't like conflict.

I wanted to go home but trudged into the bedlam to search for my friends. They had spread a blanket on the ground near a TV news van and were sitting cross-legged in a circle. Their eyes were already closed, their faces barely visible between pulled-down caps and pulled-up collars. Without greeting them, I tiptoed across the circle and claimed the cushion they'd saved for me. The blanket beneath us offered little protection from the still-frozen earth of early spring. The wind, damp and raw, sliced right through my sweater. The odor of exhaust blew in from the street. I shoved my hands into my pockets and hunched my shoulders.

The crowd swirled around us. They tramped across the corners of our quilt. I shivered from both the discord and the cold.

I closed my eyes to meditate. Alone in the dark. Voices thundered above me. I felt an abrupt tug on the blanket, heard a surprised "What the—" and then sensed the vibration of retreating footsteps. Hostile exchanges grew louder and closer.

"... your freedom, assholes..."

"... bullshit."

It sounded like two couples. They shrieked their arguments at each other as though they were tossing grenades. I ducked.

Randy shouted above the laughter and music that enveloped us. "What were you thinking?"

I had posed the same question. How can a person show support for peace? When a friend suggested we meditate at the rally, my heart recognized the answer. When I sat on the ground and closed my eyes, my mind disagreed. *They're going to kill us. I'm starving. How much longer?*

I tried to concentrate. *Focus on the inhale. Focus on the exhale.* I followed the sting of the air, in and out. Chest rising and falling. Finally, the shouting-drumming- barking-rapping abated behind the murmur of my breath.

Somewhere in the crowd, Randy was watching. He spotted us meditating in the middle of a battleground, and he took our picture. From that day until I met him more than a year later, our photo had hung in his studio. It inspired him to paint a watercolor homage.

I doubted I'd accomplished anything at all, but Randy took exception. The rally had been too contentious for him. He'd left after taking our photo.

"What you did... it really touched my heart," he said.

Our expression of peace engendered his. His painting might stir other hearts.

I had no idea one person could have such an effect on another. It made me feel like a hero: proud that my action had transformed a life, and humbled at the realization that it *could*. Alone in the dark, I'd brought light to the world.

Fun and Games

Sujata purred yoga instructions my mind could not fathom, but my body was fluent in the poetry she spoke.

Standing Forward Bend. "Lean your head back into a pillow of grace and then plunge into the river of life."

I leaned backward, arms outstretched, gaze fixed on the heavens. Just when gravity should have defeated me, an invisible force cradled my head. It nudged me upright, until I arced forward into a swan dive, then pierced the surface of the floor without a ripple, the wind whooshing past my ears.

Half Moon. "Expand into a full expression of the pose."

I balanced on my right foot and the fingertips of my right hand. My left leg, horizontal to the floor, broke through the second-story wall and hovered over the parking lot. My left arm soared through the ceiling. A passing cloud brushed my fingertip.

Warrior II. "Shoot a beam of radiant energy through your arms."

I focused, aimed, and fired. The flash burst a carton of milk in the dairy case of the store across the street.

For two hours a week my gray hair and cellulite vanished. I was Flo Jo, muscles rock solid. My locks were ponytailed during class and my fingernails trimmed short. Still, I thought of Flo Jo's wild hair streaming in her wake and her too-long-to-type-with fingernails flashing blue as she sped past all those hapless 100-meter competitors.

It mystified me that I awoke to the same thought on every yoga morning: *I don't want to go.* Still half asleep, I scanned my body for symptoms that would justify my skipping class. I cursed Sujata for remaining too fit to retire, even though she was seventy. When a snowstorm blocked the roads one morning, I rejoiced, but my husband Ben walked into the bedroom with his car keys. "You love yoga. I'll take you."

My conflict ended the night I slipped on an icy sidewalk and broke my wrist. In the emergency room, the orthopedist wound gauze around my arm from knuckles to bicep. He framed the limb in splints, which imprisoned it at a right angle. The whole thing rested across my belly in a sling, my fingers dangling from the end like squid tentacles.

I adapted without complaint. Learned to type, cook, and dress with one hand. There'd be no yoga for a few weeks, but it couldn't be helped. I gloated over my positive attitude.

I tuned the radio to the morning news, wrapped my splinted arm in a plastic bag, and headed for the shower. An unsettled feeling stopped me mid-stride between the bedroom and bathroom: the mental tickle that occurs just before recalling the name of a movie or the last place I set my glasses. A tidbit of information skulked in the shadows of awareness. I held still; any quick movement might cause the fragile impression to slip away. It flashed across my consciousness in a single sentence.

"I sabotaged yoga."

The statement crashed into my chest with a force that could not be ignored.

The newscaster droned in the background. The furnace kicked on. A sound track to memories from the night I fell on the ice. The searing pain that slashed through my arm when the frozen ground slammed into it and how I tried to seem okay as friends drove me home. And then the shock on Ben's face when he peeled off my coat, the tension in his voice. "Get in the car. We're going to the emergency room. Now."

I stared down at my arm, encased in plastic, and succumbed to alternating waves of sadness, horror, and disbelief. How could I do that to me? Yoga was fun.

> *¹fun n 1: what provides amusement or enjoyment: specif: playful often boisterous action or speech <full of ~>*

"What are you doing in here?" Sooner or later, an adult would discover me alone in my room, the only kid left in the house. "Go outside and play."

When my brothers and sister were off with their friends, I played alone in the house. When my cousins visited, I hid. They were older, street wise. They knew the latest songs and dances. Anytime Aunt Gerry came down from Cedar Rapids with her boys, or Uncle Al and Aunt Ann brought their kids over from Eighteenth Street, or Uncle Frank and Aunt Margaret dropped by with Little Frank, I stayed inside. I curled up with the latest issue of *My Weekly Reader* or crouched on the landing, trying to be invisible, eavesdropping on the adults. They told stories on each other as they slapped cards and drank gin in the kitchen. When the cussing got fast and shrill, I shrank into the woodwork.

Mama and Dad ignored me, but eventually my silent presence annoyed one of the aunts or uncles. "What are you doing in here? Go outside and play."

Outside. In the summer, boys hurled buckeyes at me, and the Iowa heat raised an itchy rash between my fingers. In the winter, those boys threw snowballs laced with rocks, and icy wind burned my toes. All year round, a pack of German shepherds prowled the neighborhood. One of them attacked me on my way home from school, just as I turned up our driveway. He clamped his fangs onto my shirttail. Growled. Shook his slobbery snout until a passing car grabbed his attention. After he trotted off, I was left trembling in the drive, discarded prey, unable to shake off the smell of dog.

Play. Kids from around the block organized baseball games in the field behind our house or hide-and-seek in the street. I lurked on the outskirts, too slow to be a valuable teammate, too naïve to understand the joking. My attempts to play ended with me in tears, done in by a skinned knee or bruised feelings.

"What's wrong with *her*?"

"Who cares? Crybaby."

I hung my head, shambled home, where Aunt Gerry repeated the question. "Jesus Christ. What the hell's wrong with her? Out there only five minutes."

Inside battered my psyche just as much as outside. Sometimes we played Monopoly, each match lasting days at a stretch—for everyone but me. Faster hands than mine grabbed the best tokens; I ended up with the thimble. The banker doled out the money and by my third roll, I picked "Go Directly To Jail. Do Not Pass Go. Do Not Collect $200." My brother sold me a get-out-of-jail-free card for forty dollars. Regular stops on Boardwalk, bedecked with hotels, bankrupted me. I was the first one out of the game. A thimble stands no chance against cannons, racecars, and battleships.

Uncle Al rescued me sometimes, took me for rides in his speedboat, up the Des Moines River. He was playing hide and seek with Dad, who snuck away from home at five a.m. to go fishing. As Uncle Al carved the river into arcs, the boat bumped over its own wake. I leaned forward across the windshield, closing in on joy with every bounce. I hated finding Dad. His yellow cabin cruiser peeked out of a cove and rocked in the swells as the speedboat flew past, then doubled back, Dad's fist stabbing the air. "Goddammit, Al, you scared off the fish."

In junior high, I gained a little confidence. Talent shows sprang up everywhere: school, Brownies, even the roller rink. When our church announced a writing contest, it sounded fun. I was great at words. I'd become an avid letter writer, if only to my grandmother. She praised my wit and penmanship, but best of all, she wrote back. The sight of her script on an envelope transported me right into the living room of her house in Ottumwa. During visits, I sprawled on the carpet, while she played "Claire de Lune" on her grand piano. After dinner she stretched out on a day bed, which was pushed up against a wall in the dining room. She worked a crossword puzzle, and the news played softly in the background, every few minutes interrupted by John Deere commercials. One Sunday evening, we parked ourselves shoulder to shoulder on the edge of the bed to gawk at the Beatles on Ed Sullivan.

Writing for a contest couldn't be much different from penning a letter. Composing my entry, I was as game as a master puzzler, selected exactly the right words, scooted them around to fit just so into sentences, then paragraphs, and finally an essay—a label that bestowed my undertaking with a sense of mystery. What riddles would I solve along the way, before clipping the finished pages inside a brand new colored folder?

    On awards night, we contestants gathered on the platform in the church sanctuary. After we read our papers to the audience, a judge announced the winners. Third place to Rosie Jackson, the pastor's daughter, second to

Beverly Norman. "And first prize goes to... Dawn Downey. Congratulations, Dawn." I stepped forward, eyes wide, my hand covering the grin that stretched across my face. My parents beamed from the third row. Waves of applause rolled over me, making my skin tingle.

At the side of the platform, the judges conferred. One of them approached the microphone. "Ladies and gentleman, we've made a mistake. First place goes to Rosie and third place to Dawn."

It knocked the breath out of me. My cheeks burned. I wanted to squeeze my eyes shut, but willed them to stay open, to hold back the moisture that was pooling in the corners. I bit my bottom lip, held in the shame in order to hold myself erect.

The winner took her place; I slipped into her shadow.

The years blurred into a montage of never-knowing-how. How to play spades with my college suitemates. How to dance without men mistaking my undulations for invitations. How to cook for the sheer delight of it.

Thirty years old and sick of my always-say-no self, I made plans to attend a concert with a group of co-workers. I spent the day shopping for a dress, and for dinner grabbed the remnants of a pineapple-Canadian bacon pizza my roommate had left on the kitchen counter.

After we settled into our seats, my companions passed around a pint of whiskey. We drank it straight, from paper cups. Midway through the performance, I rushed to the bathroom and slammed the stall door behind me. I kneeled on the concrete just in time to heave the pizza and alcohol into the toilet. The stall spun. I collapsed onto the seat and crumpled over, head between my knees. When I opened my eyes, I was being hauled like a corpse through the lobby. One of the men had hooked his hands under my armpits, while another hoisted me by the legs. A minute later, or maybe an hour, maybe a week, I was lying on my bed, the walls swaying around me.

fun adj 1: providing entertainment, amusement, or enjoyment <a ~ person to be with>
(Merriam-Webster)

I sabotaged yoga. I slumped in the chair, hoping to find answers by staring at my arm. My shoulder ached from the weight of the splint. I staggered across the room, switched off the radio, and then climbed into the shower to sort things out.

What's wrong with me? My friends were fun. Nancy joined her sister's fiftieth birthday celebration, white-water rafting down the Colorado River. Stef and Doug took off for weekend bicycle rides, pulling a pop-up tent behind one of their bikes. Kate played in her backyard, pampering a collection of exotic plants under the watchful eyes of her garden gnomes and faeries.

And Ben. We were driving across Missouri, on our way home from a retreat. My attention floated above the soybean fields until his voice brought me back. "Look at that. A crop of commercial sunflowers."

A blur of scraggly brown discs sped past.

I rotated in my seat to keep them in view. "Huh. Never thought of them as crops."

"Want to see them up close?"

"Really? Yeah."

I'd assumed the moment would pass. He'd remember the emails and phone calls he needed to return. Instead, he whipped a U-turn at the next exit and winked at me. "There's always time to play."

The orthopedist removed my cast two weeks earlier than scheduled. Amazed at my speedy recovery, he asked, " Do you exercise?"

"Yoga," I said.

He nodded. "People who practice yoga heal faster."

[3] ***fun*** *adj: providing amusement, entertainment or enjoyment* (Merriam-Webster)

"Find the joy in your practice." Sujata's first instruction on my first day back.

I'd risen from bed that morning without the usual search for symptoms, but I'd misplaced the joy. My wrist was too weak to support Downward Facing Dog, and halfway through class I needed a pillow of grace to prop up my sore arm.

"Face the window for standing poses."

The warrior queen perked up. She squared her stance. Feet planted, she armed herself with a beam of radiant energy. A tank of unleaded at the corner gas station in her sights, a glorious explosion imminent.

Sujata glided around us, examining our postures, touching a spine here, a shoulder there. As she floated past, her fingertips lingered feather-soft on my wounded wrist, encouraged my arm to straighten. I tracked her circuitous route around the room by the shifting location of her voice. The soprano lilt stopped. The silence was interminable.

The warrior queen grew restless.

I glanced toward the front of the studio and was embarrassed to discover Sujata watching me.

"It's wonderful," she said, "to look out and see Dawn smiling."

The *N* Word:
A Prayer of Thanksgiving

Dessert plates cluttered my coffee table. Candles flickered hypnotic shadows, the waxy scent a complement to the mingled aromas of Riesling and rosé. I lounged in my living room on Thanksgiving night with members of my meditation group, our dharma discussions set aside for an evening while we gossiped about politicians and celebrities.

Ted perched on the edge of an overstuffed chair, erect as a monk. Opera was his avocation, although he also composed chants and wrote poetry. Whenever the acoustics of a room tempted him, he sang an Italian aria. It was always a treat for me to watch as he fell in love with the music.

Rhonda snuggled into the couch. Her hand caressed the velvet as she lamented her unsuccessful attempts to find a girlfriend. I admired her sense of style, from clothes to gardens to interiors. We often met for lunch, where we explored the secret corners of our lives, all the hurts that had turned us each into spiritual seekers.

A married couple squeezed next to her on the sofa, and Ted's wife curled up in a chair.

That week the Internet buzzed with gossip about a white stand-up comic who had shouted racial slurs at black hecklers. We shook our heads and tut-tutted his behavior.

Our comments remained a safe distance from our personal feelings.

"... can't imagine what he was thinking."

"... showed his ignorance."

"... worse than the hecklers."

Still, I squirmed a bit; I was the only black person in the room.

I set my rocking chair in motion with my foot.

Ted folded his hands in his lap and bowed his head to study them. He raised his gaze, seeming to look at nothing in particular. "My dad was racist. He called his employees niggers."

The word seared me like a hot poker.

I stopped rocking.

I stared at his face, unable to turn away, not wanting to draw attention to my embarrassment. His expression gave away no sign that he worried about my reaction... no sign that he cared about me. If only he would flinch.

He didn't. He continued as if he'd only said, "My father called them names."

It sounded like he'd used that word 10,000 times before. Why did he think he could say it in my house?

Rhonda wrapped her arms around a chenille pillow. "Yeah, my dad, too. Nigger, all the time."

What? My tongue turned into a thick, dry lump. Hands went cold, face hot. I braced myself, certain the first two blows portended a third.

Speak up, Dawn. I wanted someone else to rescue me from the assault. But why should they? I was just a nigger.

If only the evening could rewind to fifteen minutes earlier, back when I was safe and my companions were innocent. No longer friends, they became *them*, people from whom I needed protection.

In college, my black classmates—who'd grown up imprisoned in the inner city—insisted, "You can't trust white people. No way. No how." I disagreed with them, since half my relatives, at least by marriage, were white. Younger brother. Baby sister. Stepmother. Maternal great grandmother. And the Downey who probably owned my paternal great-great-grandfather. As I grew older, I became less trusting. I suspected all (most? some? how do you arrive at an estimation?) white people sprinkled their chitchat with racial slurs, within the confines of their private circles. My suspicion congealed as I attended on-the-job diversity workshops and after-work cocktail parties. It seemed the more I got to know acquaintances who were white, the closer I got to a danger zone... where they forgot... perhaps... that a black person was in the room. And then a racist comment slipped out. What shattered me was the ease with which it slipped.

Thanksgiving night's small talk drifted by, through the fog of my shame. It trailed off and my dinner party lumbered to an end.

The scene haunted me. Ted's dour expression. Rhonda hugging my pillow.

Day after day, I waited for one of the others who'd been present to call and say, "I'm sorry Rhonda and Ted were so insensitive." Or "Hope you're okay." After all, maybe they'd been afraid to voice their sympathy that night, and maybe they'd find the courage in a faceless telephone call or email. But I was deluding myself, assuming kindness where there had been only silence. And then I waited for my anger to rise. Wouldn't I feel better after throwing something? At whom? Rhonda and Ted, for saying it? Me, for not speaking up? I was alone. No allies. No enemies.

I lay in bed, preoccupations eclipsing into sleep. Although buried under a comforter, I shuddered, and the rage erupted in waves. I screamed into my pillow. Thrashed. Clenched my gut and moaned. My tangled bedding was damp with tears and sweat. It would never end. I would never be safe.

Hopeless.

You get there by sinking.

I sank through a quagmire of shackles, chains, branding irons, whips, ropes, nightsticks, burning crosses, and fire hoses. Bloodhounds on my trail, police dogs at my throat. Crashed through all the places that are supposed to be safe: school yards, lunch counters, courthouses, and church basements. From nigger to nigra to colored to negro to black to african-american. One meaningless label after another, each meant to hold me apart as the other. Right back to the beginning. Strange fruit.

The storm subsided. On the other side of hopeless, there was silence.

I got up, washed my face, and then climbed back into bed. Just before drifting off to sleep, I knew.

Shit. I have to talk to them.

The Buddha said, "Take refuge in the sangha." A double paradox. First, "the sangha" had ambushed me on Thanksgiving. Second, I doubt the great teacher intended refuge as a place of safety. He would have shaken his head at the notion of protecting myself.

The members of my meditation group shared a single bond: curiosity about the Ultimate Mystery. No common personalities, life experiences, or family histories bound us to one another. We all sought Truth, and yet our values were different. We were bound to clash.

The Buddha did not advise me to turn away from conflict. His teachings assured that if I examined my experiences, good and bad, I'd discover something pure. Even challenged me to look for myself, rather than accepting the teachings untested. I was compelled to look, compelled to unravel the Mystery.

Rhonda and I went out to dinner. We'd scheduled the date weeks before Thanksgiving. After dinner, she would accompany me to a magazine launch, where she'd be my cheerleader while I read. I pushed my food around the plate, pleased she wanted to support my performance, but also worried about broaching the subject of the *N* word. She might protest or label me hypersensitive. I could end up feeling worse.

"Not sure how to say this. Thanksgiving night... I felt attacked... you said..."

"Oh God." She gasped. She clenched her gut. "I feel like that when somebody says 'dyke.'"

We winced from a single stab of pain. Her word encompassed all the slurs I'd overheard, as well as those to which my own ignorance had given voice. She touched my hand. "I'm so sorry."

Neither of us moved, even our breath too quiet to trouble the peaceful space that held us.

She nodded, smiling. "Thank you."

I approached Ted after a Sunday morning meditation.

"Remember Thanksgiving? What you said... it hurt me... still hurts."

He towered over me by a foot. "I certainly didn't mean to. I'm sorry if I did." His eyes betrayed no emotion.

I walked away, disappointed, but resigned. I'd done my best. In fact, the apology was his best, too. Time to let it go.

After an evening discussion group, he tapped me on the arm. I turned to face him. His eyes brimmed with tears. His voice cracked. "You really got to me. That night I was talking about my dad, but I see myself. It's painful. Realizing how hard my heart is. I'm deeply sorry... and I want to thank you."

His face was flushed, but his gaze was soft. Encircled by empty chairs and the bustle of departing friends, we recognized each other.

It would never end. I'd never be safe. And yet, the gratitude Rhonda and Ted expressed had enveloped me as well. I was mystified. In the collision of our three lives, I discovered something pure: an alchemy that transformed profanities into prayers of thanksgiving.

Anicca:
How I Escaped from Maniacal Meditators

I stepped through the door of the meditation hall and added my shoes to the growing pile. In the crowded entryway, I bumped heads with a woman wearing a neon orange tracksuit, mouthed a 'scuze me, and moved on.

It was the first day of a ten-day retreat, led via videotape by a popular Indian teacher (hereafter referred to as "PI Teacher"). The interior walls of a ranch house had been removed to create a space big enough to squeeze in a hundred meditators, males and females separated by a center aisle. A raised platform ran the length of the room along one wall. Zafus and zabutons formed well-disciplined rows on the floor in front of it, reserved for veterans of PI Teacher's previous courses. Behind them, heaps of sofa cushions, folded blankets, and floor pillows comprised the newbie section. Chairs lined the back wall, for those of us too inflexible to sit on the floor. Every spot bore a placard with a student's name on it.

I claimed my assigned chair and tucked a shawl under my feet.

In previous years, I'd performed that ritual countless times in a meditation hall where my sangha met. I relished the routine of silent retreats. The familiar rustle as we each settled into a not-quite-comfortable position. Our teacher, attired in khakis and polo, greeting us with a gentle, "Good evening, friends." On the first night, he usually led us in an abbreviated twenty-minute sit and sent us—travel weary—off to bed. The real work started on the second day. Meditation from sunrise to moonrise (blessedly silent, except for the warble of tree frogs). Breaks for meals. Evening dharma talk, followed by group discussion. Fall into bed at ten.

The squeak of a screen door brought me back to the present as a rush of heat displaced the air-conditioned chill. Autumn sunshine spotlighted our facilitator in the doorway. Fair-skinned and blonde, he tiptoed around pillows and outstretched legs. His white robes billowed as he made his way to the platform.
Robes?
Without introducing himself, he popped a videocassette into an audio-visual system and dimmed the overhead lights. I assumed it was dramatic flair; surely the *good evening, friends* would come later.

PI Teacher's flickering image materialized on two television monitors. His horn-rimmed glasses framed deep-set black eyes. White hair, ever-present grin, and chubby cheeks gave him an impish appearance. Deep furrows played across his golden skin when he spoke. "Seek happiness only inside yourself, because everything outside changes. Resistance to this truth is madness. Surrender to—"

Thud. A brunette hardly a hairbreadth away from my shawl-wrapped toes plopped onto all fours and waggled her bottom back and forth. She situated herself on a stack of blankets, then rose and tried a chair, and finally folded her legs beneath a bench.

I shifted to get a better view of PI Teacher's face.

Two stations east of Lady Waggler, a pony-tailed woman

vibrated. Leaning back on her elbows, her legs crossed at the knees, she bounced one shin up and down like a piston.

On the monitor, the videotaped audience leaned in with rapt attention as PI Teacher lectured.

Something sputtered to my left. The noise emanated from a spot where sofa cushions, blankets, and beanbag pillows surrounded an orange-clad matron in a beach chair. The lady I'd bumped heads with. Madame Tracksuit picked up a pillow, threw it onto the floor, tenderized it with her fist, shoved it under her knee, and repeated the violence with the other pillow.

I'd settled into my spot with minimal fuss; I was a pro. The muscles at the base of my neck tightened at the prospect of sitting among these amateurs.

Laugh lines danced around PI Teacher's eyes. His Indian lilt transformed his words into music. "Resistance is madness."

The dharma talk ended two hours later, with the guru bowing low to his audience.

Back in real life, our facilitator flicked on the lights. I waited for the discussion to begin. Instead, he said, "We'll meet again at nine a.m. Take rest." He swept out of the room.

We marched back to our dorm, a long, low building with a single hallway that opened into two-bedroom suites. I opened the door into my suite's closet-sized entry and stopped in the bathroom to wash my face. Strands of long brown hair—not mine—clung to the sides of the sink. As I was debating whether to swear at them or wash them down the drain, a shadow crossed the threshold. I peeked through the door, which was ajar. Lady Waggler. Let her clean up her own hair.

At four o'clock in the morning we trekked from the dorm to the meditation hall for an optional pre-dawn sitting. Cornstalks in a field bordering the pathway witnessed our journey. I'd never walked through a night so black and still. Even the sky was asleep.

The magic wore off inside the hall. Four a.m. was a nice place to visit, but I sure couldn't live there. As soon as my eyes closed, I dozed off.

The involuntary nap didn't help. After breakfast, PI Teacher's disembodied voice emanated from wall-mounted speakers, no video. He instructed us to focus on the sensation of the breath passing over the tip of the nostrils.

I felt the sensation of sleep overtaking me.

Again.

Drowsiness was interrupted by sounds I hadn't heard since we put a new roof on our house. Lady Waggler was dragging her furniture collection to the back row. She destroyed three meditation stations along the way, which set off a chain reaction of reconstruction.

Obviously, she doesn't know how to ignore her discomfort. I attacked my search for peace with renewed resolve, rubbing my tight shoulders.

PI Teacher continued his lesson. "The mind—"

Ms. Pony Tail popped her chewing gum.

"—spends most of the time lost in fantasies—"

Wasn't there a Carol Burnett episode about bubble gum?

"—and anticipating the future—"

I'll Google it next week when I get home.

"—never realizing the peace that—"

Geez, did somebody just belch?

While we meditated, PI Teacher chanted prayers of compassion in a relentless monotone. I prayed he'd stop.

He repeated rote instructions. "Focus on your breathing." "Watch your breath." "Follow the inhale." His accent made it difficult to discern if he'd switched from English to the Buddha's native Pali. I could meditate in peace if only he'd quit.... oh... respiration. I thought he'd said observe my desperation.

The evening videos of his dharma talks compensated for the hard work of each day. Gestures and sound effects highlighted his lectures. "It's the law of impermanence, anicca." It sounded like a sneeze. Ah-neé-chah. "Everything you desire and all that you seek to avoid will change." He relayed the dharma like someone telling his favorite joke, chortling all the way to the punch line. "Seek happiness only inside yourself."

Night after night, the lights came up, signaling the familiar question-and-answer session. I wanted to ask, Why was PI Teacher laughing? But night after night, our facilitator gathered his robes around him and dumbfounded me with the same two words. "Take rest."

Returning to my room for an afternoon shower, I stifled a screech when a grasshopper flew past my face. A second one sent me leaping into the corn. I looked around to make sure no one had seen me. Once in the bathroom, I pulled back the shower curtain. A cricket strolled across a mat of hair in the tub. *Dammit.* I opted to "take rest," but a nap proved out of the question too, because another cricket hopped from a corner of my bedroom and hid under the desk. I had to get out of there. Nature belonged on television, not jumping up all around me.

PI Teacher's recorded voice challenged us to remain motionless for an hour. Finally, the silent retreat was silent.

But during the breaks, Madame Tracksuit (in metallic white) remodeled. By dinnertime, she'd transformed her pile of pillows into a lounge chair, complete with headrest, footstool, and cup holders.

If I could sit still, why couldn't she? Why couldn't any of them? I glared holes in the motionless backs of the zafu-sitters, who reposed in lotus at the front, oblivious to the suffering at the rear. Who did they bribe for their luxury seats in the quiet section?

PI Teacher instructed us to spend two days observing the various itches, twinges, tingles, prickles, and chills that erupted throughout our bodies. The class moved on without me. I was still trying to locate feelings in my nose. "Meditate no matter what you're doing. Do everything with awareness."

Ms. Pony Tail drummed her fingers on the hardwood floor. I gritted my teeth, with awareness.

Lady Waggler's hair accumulated in the tub. I smacked the shower curtain, with awareness.

I fell into bed, exhausted, but couldn't sleep. A cricket was hiding somewhere in my room. I cringed at the chirping, with awareness.

Ms. Pony Tail's zabuton invaded the spot previously occupied by my feet. With my jaw clenched, I nudged her to point out she'd trespassed on pre-owned real estate. She bowed in apology and smiled when she pulled her mat away from my chair.

Her sweet demeanor startled me; I'd expected an exasperated sigh. I glanced away. We were packed in shoulder to shoulder. It was impossible to claim a spot that didn't violate your neighbor's personal space, yet no one's face registered the annoyance that twisted mine into a grimace. I was beginning to feel like Attila the Hun at a peace rally.

Oh. *Those* sensations at the tip of the nostrils. Who would have guessed there was so much going on in the nose?

Lethargy dissipated just long enough for me to taste what I'd been missing. A sweet spot, popping with life: an itch, an air current passed over my cheek, an airplane droned in the distance, a fly buzzed, a mental picture of the dining hall flashed, an opinion emerged from nothingness—evaporated just shy of completing itself. All of it devoid of time. My sweet spot turned sour when somebody started sniffling, every thirty seconds, steady as a metronome. The gloppy breathing made me long for the indifference of sleep. I felt a new sensation: the ache in my shoulders traveling down my back.

A long hot shower would help. With any luck, my roommate might have cleaned the bathroom. No luck. A cricket perched on the mat hanging across the tub. Strands of hair slithered down the side. Without thinking about it, I folded the mat around the cricket, took it outside and set the critter free. The door to our suite open mid-swing, doorknob still in my grasp, it occurred to me what I'd just done. Or somebody had done it. God knows, I'd never gotten that close to a bug. Not on purpose, anyway. It would add a cheery surprise if Lady Waggler cleaned her hair out of the tub.

Seek happiness inside yourself.

The bathroom mirror reflected a face hardened into a scowl. That was not a happy woman. A wave of sadness washed away my irritation. I swished Lady Waggler's hair down the drain with a blast of water from the showerhead, then stepped into the stream and blasted the tension from my lower back.

A hubbub after dinner delayed the start of the evening session. Retreat staff signaled to each other. They counted the cushion piles, tried the bathroom door. One of them left the hall.

Geez. Now what?

She returned with Lady Waggler, who lumbered to her spot. She winced when she curled onto her chair. Her face contorted.

That sound, that look. I'd groaned like that for weeks after spraining a knee. Pain had contorted my features when it sliced through the injured joint. *This poor woman hurts.* I sent her metta.

"How you doin'?" Madame Tracksuit approached on the pathway, adorned in iridescent lavender. Her close-cropped hair looked painted on, with c-shaped spit curls in front of her ears. "This is intense, and I have a feeling it's going to get worse."

Why's she talking to me at a silent retreat?

"My daughter got me into this," she said.

"You ever meditate before?"

"No. If you hear somebody screaming, that's me."

I chuckled in sympathy. "Thanks for the warning."

She was learning meditation by doing it ten hours straight for ten days in a row. No flesh-and-blood teacher to offer a "good work, you're on the right track." My resolve paled next to hers. She sped off, and I shout-whispered after her, "Good luck."

One day remained before we broke the silence. Surely our mute facilitator would offer instructions. I plodded to the meditation hall, anticipating the sound of a voice other than PI Teacher's. A sign hung on the door. *Silence will end at 9 a.m. tomorrow.* It provided no details, merely dangled the hope of a commuted sentence.

After breakfast the following day, Madame Tracksuit (in glow-in-the-dark pink) caught up with me again. "New instructions for today," she said. "We can talk pretty soon."

I patted her on the shoulder. "You must be pretty happy."

She nodded. "But it's been good. It's good to get quiet." She scurried away.

At 9 a.m., the atmosphere in the meditation hall was coiled in anticipation, although the facilitator relaxed in royal ease on his Zabuton. He leaned forward, certainly about to congratulate the group on a great retreat. Wrong. Without so much as a glance in our direction, he turned off the sound, monitors, lights, and air conditioning. Straightened his robes around him and tiptoed out of the house. No one moved—until Madame Tracksuit leaped to her feet and yelled, "Thank you Jesus! It's over."

The room erupted. Newbies in the back squealed, chattered, and giggled, while stoic veterans in front greeted each other with namasté. Mass hugging erased the aisle that previously separated damsels from dudes. The mob spilled out into the parking lot like a flock of geese descending on a pond. I was stunned, used to the hushed tones of a formal closing circle, in which we reflected on how we'd experienced the week, what insights we'd gained about ourselves. But this... the sound was too intense, the change too abrupt. I felt assaulted.

A woman wrapped in a shawl escaped to a bench away from the crowd, an empty seat beside her. I inched closer. "Is this taken?"

"No. Sorry, I'm not very talkative. This part's always too jarring for me."

"Always? You've done this retreat before?"

"Three times."

"What do you get from it?"

"I keep seeing how crazy my mind is. Can't believe it's in charge of my life."

At lunchtime, I trudged to the dining hall. I must have misread the schedule. I must have miscounted the days. A sign posted next to the double door ordered us back into the silence for the following morning.

Another day? Back into the silence? No.

I pushed on the door. It stuck. I pushed with my shoulder. Nothing. Leaned into it. It didn't budge. Madame Tracksuit, in fire engine red, came up from behind, hugged me, and breezed through the unlocked side. The door slapped shut behind her.

Laugh lines danced around PI Teacher's eyes. "Resistance is madness."

Well, why didn't you tell me that ten days ago?

I followed Madame Tracksuit into the noisy dining hall. She told me her daughter had taken PI Teacher's course the year before. "She was so calm afterward. She paid for me to take it, too. Thought it would help my tension headaches." By the end of dinner, I'd met them all. Lady Waggler had strained her back right before the retreat but wanted to come anyway. Ms. Pony Tail was just out of college, but she'd already taken the course twice before.

As I walked to the last session, a grasshopper landed square on my chest, head pointed at mine. I stopped. It seemed the most natural thing in the world to peer into his bulging eyes, as though I chatted with grasshoppers on a regular basis. The world shrank down to the two of us, neither one twitching, no destination other than this patch of dirt, until he hopped into the cornfield.

During PI Teacher's recorded closing lecture, my neighbors vibrated, twitched, squirmed, coughed, muttered, and sneezed. Linda popped her gum; Georgia pounded her pillows; Patricia rubbed her aching back.

My breath eased, silky, across the tip of my nose as I closed my eyes for our final meditation. *Take rest.*

Burgers, Beer, and Emotional Baggage:
Marinate in Mindfulness before Grilling Yourself

I grabbed my straw hat from the dashboard as my husband waited beside the car, and then, my hand in his, we followed the aroma of hickory-smoked burgers to the wooden fence that enclosed our friend's back yard.

After a daylong retreat, I anticipated Kate's barbecue like a kid looking forward to recess. My mind had slowed during meditation, to contemplate the touch sensation of each breath, to wonder at the miracle of dust particles floating in the sunbeams that angled in through the windows. Now I was eager to speed up, to laugh too loudly and eat too much. What was the latest news about Carol's job and Barbara's reflexology class? The fellow practitioners I'd sat with all day would greet me with bear hugs or a silly *haven't seen you forever*, but when Ben opened the gate and stood aside to let me go in first, no one waved a welcoming hello. A crowd of poker-faced strangers filled the yard.

I froze, thrown back in time, slammed into a younger version of myself, when other stony countenances barred my way.

The Christmas after Mama and Dad divorced, Uncle Al and Aunt Ann planned a family gathering. They invited Mama, although Dad was expected with his new wife. "You can't stay home alone on Christmas, Catherine."

The house was loud with cousins, siblings, aunts, uncles, and neighbors. When Dad and Kim came through the front door, Mama snuck through the kitchen doorway down to the basement, to watch television in a makeshift bedroom near the furnace. Surreptitiously, I studied the faces around the table, searching for a sympathetic glance in her direction. Listened for the slightest sigh of acknowledgement that she'd been cast out, and then followed her, intending to keep her company.

"Mama?"

No answer.

I reached the bottom step. "Mama?"

She was reclining in an overstuffed chair in front of the television. Silhouetted against the flickering screen, she registered no awareness of my presence, her profile pale and motionless.

I crept across the concrete floor, cold leaching through my thin-soled shoes, and stopped next to her. I could not divine an emotion in the carefully tweezed curve of her brow. Was she sad? Outraged? Did she blame me? "Mama?"

Laughter filtered down from the kitchen. Dad probably repeating one of his funny stories, or teasing Aunt Ann—proclaiming she was too good for Uncle Al.

If I plopped down at Mama's feet, leaned my shoulder against her calf, maybe she'd forgive me for not protecting her from this humiliation. It was my fault. Hadn't I been eavesdropping from the couch when Uncle Al invited her? Hadn't I failed to state the obvious—spending Christmas with your ex-husband's new wife was worse than spending it alone? Hadn't I failed her? Maybe I should pat her shoulder instead, but what if she smacked my hand away, while her eyes bored hatred into mine? There was no tilt of her head to guide me either toward action or inaction, not that night or all the nights before. I crept back upstairs, too late to get in on Dad's joke. Mama stayed in the basement, an invisible weight tethered to my ankles.

Dad transplanted our family—five kids and his new wife—from Iowa to California, where I was the new girl in high school. Returning to the building at the end of lunch hour, I ran a gauntlet of poker-faced strangers, classmates who lined the sidewalk. Their dull eyes dismissive, when I dared to look. A few boys flirted. Not knowing how to play along, I ignored them. Their voices hardened. "That's how it is, sister?" "Can't even say hello?" "Stuck up." Girls spat comments about my Angela Davis afro. "Got 'em with that head, didn't you?" They waggled fingers at me. One of them closed in. "High yellow bitch." The words were opaque, but the threat transparent. I folded my arms across my chest and willed myself not to run, purse bumping against my hip with every step.

Poised with Ben at the edge of a sea of veiled faces, I was an intruder, a high yellow bitch. There was no way into the secret world the faces guarded and no clear path to safety. On top of being afraid, I was a failure, too. Week after week, I'd followed my Buddhist mindfulness instructions. *Be present with your feelings. Don't justify them; don't criticize them. Don't decide what to do about them. Only watch.* Three years, ten retreats, and 1,000 meditations into my spiritual practice, I was still dragging around emotional baggage from my teenage years.

    That tenth-grade urge to bolt welled up, but Ben blocked my path. He seemed calm, even though I accidentally stepped on his foot. "Where you going?"

I couldn't admit my terror. "Uh, nowhere. You recognize anybody?"

"Christine over by that tree. The last person I want to talk to. Maybe there's more inside."

He strolled into the yard, me gripping his hand.

A man by the grill pointed and yelled, "Burgers over here. Beer's in the cooler. Food in the kitchen."

Inside, Barbara and Carol were filling their plates at the buffet tables. I rushed at them, my arms flung open. "So great to see you guys."

Barbara, knocked off balance by my hug, dropped her spoon. "Just saw you an hour ago. What's the big deal?"

I ignored the question, because the answer embarrassed me. I kept the two of them in sight, while piling my plate with junk food. In the process, I lost track of Ben.

Abandoned.

A fresh wave of panic rolled over me. I walked out the door, trying to remember what it was like to be a confident adult. Barbara and Carol followed, but, hell, they might ditch me, too. Empty chairs remained near several partiers, their chatter peppered with spirited hoots. I joined them, balanced my plate on my knees, and looked up just in time to see my friends heading off in another direction.

I watched in disbelief, my feet anchored to the ground. The scene closed in on me, disembodied voices ringing in my ears. The strangers would call me stuck up if I left. They'd call me a bitch if I stayed.

I needed to snap out of it, search for a way back to normalcy. I waited for an opportunity to introduce myself but found nothing to add to their debate about the local college football team. No one offered an opening, so I settled into not fitting in, plastered an expression of interest on my face, and tried to ignore the smell of beer warming in the sun.

"Hey, Dawn."

I turned. Carol, Barbara, and Ben had set up four chairs under a shade tree. They motioned for me to join them. We formed a little circle of muteness. Barbara and Carol were both quiet types. Ben and I were often the entertainment, but he was busy eating, and I was busy being miserable. I kicked off a sandal and kneaded the grass with my toes. My chewing sounded deafening.

"Ben. Dawn." Kate waved at us from the other side of the yard. She dragged a chair over and parked it beside Ben. "I didn't see you come in."

Ben voiced my confusion. "I'm surprised I don't know these people. Who are they?"

"Mostly Randy's friends." She glanced toward her husband, who was just emerging from the house. "Guys he goes hunting with. Their wives. But there's some other people you all know."

Ben nodded, satisfied with her explanation.

Christine strolled over and waited to get his attention. When he failed to notice her, she turned to me. "Oh. You're here too?" It sounded like an accusation, but I smiled up at her and extended my hand. She didn't take it.

"I see you're wearing a hat—so you can hide." She arched an eyebrow and sauntered off.

I gasped, smile still painted on my face, hand still extended. The worst thing that could happen, did happen: public humiliation. She'd outed me as a fraud and branded me unacceptable. She'd exposed a nerve that twanged with the suspicion she was right. I wanted to hide, hoped no one had overheard.

In the past, my mind would have resounded with opinions. About her: obnoxious. About me: pathetic. I waited for the familiar voices, for the noise that would obscure my feelings. Silence. Not a word. Not a thought. A chasm opened between my shame and me, as though a movie camera had pulled back from a close-up to a panoramic view.

The backside of my attacker receded. Heat flooded my cheeks. My heart pounded, fast and loud. But, at the same time, I felt peaceful, even curious. I was meeting an emotion for the first time. *So... you're shame. I've heard a lot about you.*

I turned to Carol, excited about describing this miracle. "The weirdest thing just happened. Christine insulted—"

"Did I tell you the latest about my stupid job?" she asked.

What the heck. I'm talking here. I angled closer, ready to pounce. I intended to point out she'd interrupted me and hurt my feelings and what kind of Buddhist friend was she, anyway? But, really, I leaned in with the intention of feeling better, after saying all that to her.

My intention fizzled. For some inexplicable reason, it was okay to *not* feel better. Again, agitated and calm all at once. Bewildered by their coexistence. I relaxed in my chair and observed the three of us: Carol, my pissy mood, and me.

A couple strolled over, hand in hand. The woman beamed like a new bride. She pushed a wayward silver curl behind her ear.

"Hi, everybody. This is Herman."

She patted his chest. "We were friends in junior high. Got together last month at our fortieth reunion. Then he flew out to visit me, and we haven't spent a day apart."

Herman grinned from under a cowboy hat. He released her hand and put his arm around her shoulders. "Yup."

They radiated happiness—with each other, unexpected romance, a sense of unlimited possibility. It was as infectious as a baby's coo.

Once again, a distance opened between my emotion and me, yet I sensed it more intensely. I tasted delight, as never before. Neither cynicism nor jealousy diminished its sweetness. Self-centered concerns did not water it down. No disappointment that I hadn't felt it earlier, no yearning for it to last all evening, no fear that it wouldn't. Undiluted joy: an orange eaten straight from the tree.

I'd studied mindfulness with the zeal of a fanatic. Contemplations. Exercises. Verses composed of impenetrable phrases. "Arising and passing away." "In the hearing, just the heard." "Contemplate the body in the body." I didn't remember any of it at the barbecue, and I was unprepared for the firsthand experience. The way that awareness, uncaused and unavoidable, drifted in and out on a cloud of hickory smoke. The way it revealed a sense of well-being right there in the heat of my emotions, moods that proved as ephemeral as each breath I'd been taught to focus on. I suspected the only constant was the peace of mind. Unreasonable. Timeless. Reaching back, embracing adolescent me.

Truth Transcends the Facts:
A Hoax Unveils the Nature of Reality

The pain in my shoulders sliced through the tranquility of the meditation hall. It was nine o'clock in the evening. With breaks for meals and evening tea, we'd sat since five thirty in the morning. I tensed in anticipation of the sound of the bell, which would signal the end of the session.

We were midway through a ten-day silent retreat at the Bhavana Society Monastery and Meditation Center. The December cold of West Virginia's Appalachians penetrated the walls. In contrast, a soft glow emanated from the front of the hall, where a 700-pound golden Buddha dominated the altar. Buddha dwarfed three candles burning in front of him and a vase of fresh flowers at his feet. Yellow pine beams framed the altar and soared skyward to support the room's arched ceiling.

In the candlelight, thirty-five retreatants sat on cushions on the floor or on chairs at the back of the room—men on the left, women on the right. On the edge of a seat beside the door, I resisted the urge to fidget and fought off thoughts of bed. As I brought attention back to my breath one more time, a low tone from the bell rewarded my efforts. Tension eased. Shadowy figures shifted, and the hall came to life with the rustle of weary meditators stretching, twisting, and relaxing.

Someone cracked a stiffened joint. Someone else coughed. We folded our blankets, buttoned our sweaters, and pulled on our hats, preparing to traipse to our rooms. And then we waited.

Custom dictated that lay people remain in the hall until after monastics had left. Four monks and three nuns had meditated with us. In slow motion, they untucked themselves, prostrated three times before the altar, and rose gracefully to their full height. A flotilla of tall ships, six robed figures floated toward me down the long center aisle. One by one, they disappeared through the doorway.

A single monk, vice abbot Bhante Rahula, remained cross-legged on the floor at the front of the hall, still wrapped in his shawl. Several people stood and peered in his direction. Bhante sat like a stone. After a few minutes passed, many of our group walked out hesitantly. A second long pause, then others left the hall, singly and in clumps of two or three. They looked back toward the solitary figure before they passed through the door. Exhaustion cried out for me to follow.

A handful of us were left. I perched on the edge of my chair, squinting into the shadows. A suggestion of motion fluttered at the front of the room. Bhante Rahula leaned forward. He reached out as if to touch something, and then withdrew his hand into the folds of his wrap.

A bass voice rumbled through the hush. Its vibration grew into a melodic chant in an unfamiliar language, a hymn that stretched and folded back upon itself. Expanded, contracted, swelled again.

Every few minutes, I recognized an "Om." At times the chanting stopped altogether. The hall grew quiet, and then gradually, the voice returned. "Om" as *Heart Sutra*—rising from the oblivion of silence, both signifying nothing and resonant with life.

I had no idea who was chanting, what the words meant, or how long they would continue, but the sacred poetry bathed me. My pores absorbed its soothing balm, as it dissolved all traces of fatigue. My chest vibrated. My skin tingled. Curiosity evaporated, and I rested in not knowing.

When the music concluded, I felt no disappointment at its end and no hunger for its repetition. Gratitude filled the space where regret and desire usually collided.

Still seated, Bhante Rahula reached out to touch the unseen object again. He removed his shawl, folded it into a square, and laid it beside his cushion. After his prostrations, he stood with saffron robes draped loosely around him. He snuffed the flickering candles, each in turn, and his ghostly form glided down the aisle and out the door beside me.

During the course of the retreat, the monks met with the participants individually, guiding us in our practice. I was assigned to Bhante Rahula, and we met the next day. He, ramrod straight on a couch, with hands folded in his lap. I, perched on a chair facing him, intimidated by the unsmiling visage.

"Well," he said. "Do you have a question?"

The music still echoing within, I put my fist to my chest and leaned forward. "Bhante Rahula... that chant... I felt the truth... without—"

"Without knowing what the words meant. Exactly." His somber expression softened. "Three other people told me the same thing."

I thought I saw his eyes twinkle.

"Do you know who it was?" He sounded like a teenager bragging about his latest MP3 download. He didn't wait for my response. "The Dalai Lama performing a Tibetan healing chant."

Of course. The Dalai Lama would have a singing voice that sounded like God.

Then he picked up a CD sleeve from the table in front of him.

"And now it's yours," he said.

It took a second for me to realize it contained a disc of the transformative chant.

"Mine... you're giving this to me? Thank you... thank you."

It was so unexpected I forgot the questions I'd intended to ask. The interview ended with my stammered gratitude, and I headed to my room, clutching the envelope. It was difficult to walk as slowly as the monks had taught us. I wanted to skip. I wanted to celebrate. The vice abbot had given me a present. An admission ticket into an elite club of meditators who *understood*.

Once in my room, I leaned the envelope against the lamp on the dresser and noticed typing on the back.

"This is a recording of the Dalai Lama and his entourage chanting healing prayers at the sickbed of his old friend Vaclav Havel." According to the message, His Holiness had given permission for the CDs to be given away, but never sold.

I was inspired by the scene—the Dalai Lama standing beside his friend, their mutual devotion warming the room. In their willingness to share that intimacy with all of us who also needed a healing prayer, I imagined I saw Truth.

But soon after returning home to Kansas City, I plummeted from that lofty illusion in the Appalachians into the flatlands of reality.

For weeks, the Dali Lama's voice soothed my daily stress. I went to sleep to its tones. Gave copies of the CD to members of my sangha, and we meditated with the chant playing in the background.

Until a musician friend became suspicious.

He reported in an email that he'd recognized the words,

researched the recording, and uncovered its origins. The chant, he said, was not Tibetan, and the voice not the Dalai Lama's. The transcendent tones—recorded in a studio—belonged to a Dutch musician named Hein Braat. The prayer was a Hindu mantra. Maha-mrityun-jaya, a call for enlightenment.

The sickbed tale was a bedtime story.

I threw a pencil across the room. *What kind of friend destroys your fantasies? And what about me? Stupid, stupid, stupid.*

The email included a link to the artist's website. While muttering sentiments that blackened my karma for the next millennium, I tapped the return key. The web page stated the Dalai Lama story was an urban myth, which had circulated on the Internet and among meditation circles.

How could that saintly voice be Dutch and not Tibetan? Dutch—they're not even brown.

Mr. Braat was a decades-long student and practitioner of mystical chanting. Accomplished, well known, and respected across Europe. But he certainly could not list "spiritual leader of the entire world" among his credits. Who was I going to believe, a web site or a monk? A vice abbot, for crying out loud.

The site offered CDs for sale. A click on one of the icons produced a sample of Mr. Braat's voice. The sound was foggy. It failed to convince me that this was my guy. Temptation tugged at my fingers to navigate away from the site while the myth was still intact. But the Dharma insists I pay attention to this grasping after illusions. I moved the cursor to a second icon and tapped the keyboard. By the fourth note, it was clear. The familiar timbre pierced my doubt like a flaming arrow, incinerating all debate.

I surrendered.

Poor old ego. Always in danger of being made the fool. Its

determination to be right dooms it to being proven wrong. Poor old me. My obsessive search for satisfaction condemns me to a life of constant disappointment.

I clung to the notion of the Dalai Lama chanting over the sickbed of a friend. After all, that's *my* fantasy. My life's been a sickbed, and I've yearned for someone to stand beside it, kissing my hair.

Pain is certain when life reveals the stories as fiction. But if I shift the focus away from them, I can glimpse the Truth. It hides in plain sight, behind the places where it's not. It peeks around opinions and tiptoes past evidence.

Sanskrit, Tibetan, or Dutch—no language can express the Truth. Dalai Lama or Hein Braat, neither man can speak it. The facts revealed on a website are no closer to reality than the myth typed on a CD cover. Both are stories, only signs along the road. Truth is a drop of mercury. Touch it with a word, and it slips away.

Each time I hear the mantra, Truth is the peace I feel—before I label it "peace." It's my tingling skin—before I call it "tingling." It's the gratitude—before I offer a thank you. Truth *is*, before I decipher, define, or describe it.

I'll seek it now between the words. I'll doubt everything I read, question everything I assume, and reject outright everything I know for sure.

Because Truth transcends the facts.

Part III

Revelations:
Finding Myself

My face disappeared. In the bathroom mirror, I looked wrinkled. In the closet mirror, my skin was smooth. In the make-up mirror, dark circles. In the rear-view mirror, my eyes were bright. Which, if any, of those reflections was real?

The day I Skyped my sister, Michelle, her face filled my computer screen. The expressions that danced across it were mine. Our hairlines matched. Our noses, too. When she laughed, I saw my teeth. (She laughed a lot that day, and so did I.)

There's my face. Michelle's wearing it. It's beautiful.

Toadstools:
Fighting Depression, Defending the Lawn

I STARTED WEEPING in the spring. The song of a cardinal announced it was time to reclaim my warm-season ritual, a daily stroll around the park, in the cool just after sunrise. The breeze was sweet with lilac and optimism, but when a passing jogger tossed "good morning" over her shoulder, an unexpected urge to cry pinched off my response. Later at breakfast, a quick intake of breath brought on a fit of sobbing. My husband asked, "What's wrong?" I couldn't answer.

Come spring, toadstools sprouted in our front lawn. They radiated from a spot where we'd dug up a stump—roots invisible under the grass. The toadstools spoiled my plans for a perfect yard. Begonias planted at the door, liriope marching along the stairs in stripes of gold and green, vinca popping purple under an ash tree. I would create a landscape fit for Monet. Spring was for blossoms, not for agents of decay.

Moments of malaise stretched into weeks. Shadowy figures and snippets of conversation floated through the fog that eddied around me. I couldn't sort laundry into colors and whites, determine which spray bottle to pick up for dusting and which for cleaning windows, or select ingredients to combine for supper. I couldn't watch television, watched Depression instead.

Weeding out toadstools was the one chore I could manage. Simple. Monotonous. *Wrap your hands around the rake, Dawn. Drag it through the grass. Lift, reach, pull.*

At first, I only noticed them full grown, a Mongol horde in tight formation, invading the defenseless lawn. But after a few days, my trained eye detected breaks in their advancing line. I spotted them in the grass just as the crowns of their heads broke ground. Here and there a white dot poking out of the dirt. I learned to focus on the empty spaces instead of the solid mass.

Seeking fragments of normalcy, I fortified myself with caffeine. One cup of green tea equaled fifteen minutes—time enough to unload the top rack of the dishwasher. Two cups to read an email. Add Excedrin, and I could answer one.

Sometimes I escaped my jailer by reassuring Depression I was still its prisoner. "Can't possibly go to yoga," I said to the bathroom mirror, "but maybe I'll shower." *Maybe I'll put on my clothes. Maybe, pick up the car keys.*

But I missed Depression, whenever it dissipated.

Wrap your hands around the rake, Dawn. Lift, reach, pull.

After a thunderstorm, the toadstools swallowed the empty spaces. Like a lava flow, the infestation consumed fescue, violets, even dandelions unfortunate enough to spring up in its path. I was outraged. *Not my yard.* Anger ignited a spark of energy. I worked furiously, head bowed, back bent. The effort exhausted me after ten minutes.

"To hell with this." I threw the rake on the ground, then feeling sheepish, kneeled to retrieve it. Beyond my feet, the rest of the lawn: lush, emerald, glistening from the rain, indifferent to the battle I waged.

In an act of determination more than pleasure, I drove to English Landing Park, a strip of reclaimed floodplain squeezed between the Missouri River and the Burlington Northern tracks. I turned off the motor and slumped behind the wheel. The keys dangled from the ignition. I couldn't marshal strength to open the door but managed to lower the windows. A breeze brushed my face. A train whistled as it thundered through a crossing. The engine labored against a mile-long string of cars, loaded with coal from the mines of Montana. Barely visible through the windshield, the Missouri crawled east toward the Mississippi. I let the wind breathe for me. It lifted a wisp of my sorrow into the unconcerned clouds.

Wrap your hands around the rake, Dawn. Lift, reach, pull.

The toadstools and I settled into a routine. They grew. I lopped off their heads. If only I could lop off my own. Surely it was the source of all this pain.

Ben opened the bedroom door. "How're you doing, Honey?"

He was too much to take in, that he would interrupt his happy life to ask how I was doing. I started to cry.

He put his hand on my cheek. "I'm calling Phil." He went into his office to search for our therapist's number. His muffled voice on the phone offered solace.

I had faith in Phil. He would cheer me up and then, through some hocus pocus I wouldn't understand, he'd put me back together.

Perched on the edge of a chair in his office, he studied my face while I stammered out disjointed answers to his questions. He called my condition a blockage, as though I were a plumbing problem, then went straight to work unclogging it. "A child ego state," he said. "Witnessed family nightmares, too scary for a little one to handle. She hid in the shadows until now, until it was safe to cry."

She had plenty of practice not crying.

Mornings. A chronic stomachache kept me home from third grade. My parents took me to the doctor, even though Dad said I was lying to get out of going to school. "You better be sick, or…"

Days. A German shepherd leapt on me, snarling, biting, tugging my shirt with his teeth. He ran off to chase a car. I ran home. Mama was behind her closed bedroom door. Dad at work.

Nights. A monster made of chains rattled up the stairs toward my room. I hid in the closet. No point crying when I woke up. Nobody came to comfort me.

For the past few weeks Little Dawn had been bursting into tears. Finally, an explanation, an alignment of cause and effect. The logic lifted my despair. Leaving Phil's office, I assumed I was cured, but at home, the tears returned.

Despair doesn't care about logic.

I researched toadstools on the Internet: garden blogs, nursery sites, horticulture listservs.
Information gathering was based on certain imperatives:
    1) Systematize the problem
    2) Manage the process
    3) Measure the outcome
Experimentation followed, which tested the effectiveness of:
    A. Sulphate of iron
    B. Fungicide
    C. Epsom salts
Results: Failure on all counts.

I gave up on faith. At a follow-up appointment with Phil, I demanded psychotherapy, hypnotherapy, prescriptions, or at the very least, a thorough analysis replete with polysyllabic terms. "What did I witness? Can't you make me remember what happened?"

"Sometimes you don't need to know the details in order to get better." He placed a buzzer in each of my palms. "Bi-lateral stimulation," he said.

Eight syllables. Promising.

He leaned in, his eyes kind, voice soft. "I want you to take bubble baths and watch funny movies. Hold hands with Ben. You're safe now."

The reassuring tone infuriated me. It sounded patronizing, but I couldn't turn away. A little girl was watching from the dark behind my eyes.

The toadstools defeated me. My efforts collapsed under the weight of their proliferation. Returning the rake to its hook on the garage wall, I abandoned hope that the lawn would thrive again, assumed the toadstools—inevitable—would overrun it in one final assault. Instead, their numbers ebbed and flowed, one morning a cluster above the invisible root, two days later a dense carpet under the ash, and after that, a lone slender stalk near the sidewalk.

Ben was scheduled to lead a weeklong silent retreat. "I'm taking you with me," he said.

"Okay."

"You won't have to do anything—"

"Okay."

"—but I'm not leaving you here alone."

"Okay."

We slept on a twin bed. He curled around me like a cocoon.

I was resting alone in the kitchen when Lovella, the center's owner, ambled in wearing a ruffled bib apron over her dress. Just like the one Mama'd slipped over her head on long ago Saturdays, before making chili for supper, the aroma of sizzling onion stinging my nose.

Lovella's kitchen filled up with mothers, as Annette, Kate, and Bonnie padded in to prepare dinner. They floated around each other in a waltz from fridge to sink to stove. Without speaking, anticipated just when to place a dishtowel or wooden spoon into another's outstretched hand. I was lulled by squeaking cabinet doors, running water, and knives clacking against cutting boards.

Lift, reach, pull.

The mothers spoke no words of comfort the week I lived on the periphery of their retreat. But on my way to the shower, Kate wrapped her arms around me, holding on until I wilted ever so slightly into her embrace. Annette, or was it Bonnie, squeezed my hand under the table at lunch. Passing me in the hallway, Lovella patted my back. The warmth of her hand lingered after she'd gone. By week's end, depression drifted away, lifted into the silence along with the fading tones of the bell at the final meditation.

Spring turned to summer. The toadstools shriveled back underground, where they'll wait for the next good rain to push them to the surface. In my preference for the lawn, I'll scrape them away. Maybe I'll surrender to the rhythm of the task, instead of waging war. Maybe I'll remember the spring when faith made the best rake, while chopping away with logic only gave me blisters.

The Doll House

At my grandmother's, I played with a tin doll house, painted cream with green shutters and roof, the chimney planted dead center on the peak. It was a two-story model. Downstairs a living room, kitchen, and pantry. Upstairs, a bedroom opened onto a cobblestone patio. I rearranged the furniture according to my shifting moods, but always positioned the bed under a window, headboard facing the patio. I longed to shrink into that tin house, curl up on the plastic comforter, in front of windows that did not shatter.

I bent over my bed, packing for a weekend retreat. Clothes were strewn on top of the covers, a suitcase open amid the clutter. My mind wandered. From anticipation at pulling into the retreat center driveway toward the porch that overlooked well-tended gardens... to a hope that the cook had improved his vegetarian fare... to the taste of veggie burritos my sister Leslie had once fixed for me, adding so many jalapeños I begged for antacid. And hadn't Wayne mentioned her the last time we talked long distance? I straightened, cocked my head, and dropped a tee shirt mid-fold. What had he said? *Dad smacked Leslie?*

My brother had related the incident on previous occasions, but the words had aroused no curiosity. I was inured to exaggeration. Our clan language was peppered with "snatched her from here to Sunday," "like to wring her neck," and "just wanted to kill that boy." Especially when cousins and siblings reminisced about growing up with Dad and Uncle Al—Dad a disciplinarian, Uncle Al a disciple of fun. I contributed little, my recollections scant beyond fragments about visits to our grandmother's house, but I snickered on cue at the hyperbole.

As I was packing my suitcase, a figure-ground shift occurred. Unexpected, unplanned, and as effortless as releasing my grasp on a tee shirt. I had only seen the chalice, until the day the two profiles popped into view. *Smacked* wasn't hyperbole. It was fact.

I grabbed my cell phone from the nightstand. Touched green after finding Leslie's number in my contacts. "Hi, honey. How're you doing?" *Good start, Dawn. What do you say now?*

"Were you trying to get me a minute ago?" she asked. "Stupid cell is dropping calls. Thinking about switching to—"

"Dad ever hit you?"

"He gave me a black eye in fifth grade."

Oh my God! I covered my mouth, squelching an impulse to press her for details, although I prayed she would elaborate, explain why her tone of voice was telegraphing that the black eye was as mundane as a phone bill.

She said, "I'll probably stay with AT&T. It's a hassle to change."

Dad had died a dozen years earlier, but maybe it was still too soon for her to talk about it. Whatever *it* was. Maybe too soon for me to hear. I let it drop and the call plodded toward our goodbyes.

"Let's keep in touch."

"Don't wait so long."

I felt hollowed out… and puzzled by the numbness. How

could the enormity of her statement be squeezed into my limited worldview? The cell phone lay open in my hand. I set it on the nightstand, then folded the tee shirt and placed it in the suitcase.

At the retreat, I stretched out in bed, done in by a day of sitting on an unforgiving chair while trying to meditate. Mental chatter had ground to an intermittent murmur, absorbed into the steady cadence of the breath and the hourly sounding of the bell. The process was familiar, yet each retreat unfolded in its own unique manner. Sometimes, an epiphany slipped into the quiet. Always, it surprised me that sitting still brought on such deep fatigue. By bedtime, every muscle ached as it uncoiled, eased deeper into the mattress. One more breath would surely bring sleep.

Dad gave Leslie a black eye. It trailed across my consciousness like a banner.

A gasp lurched me upright. *Dad gave Leslie a black eye.*

I buried my face in the pillow and howled. Sickened by heartbreak. Pummeled by outrage I'd never felt. Tormented by a vision I couldn't make sense of. I bawled, when the howling subsided. Sobbed, when the bawling let up. *How?* I interrogated the empty room. *How does a six-foot man black a schoolgirl's eye? Did he have to bend over?* I staggered to an armchair, dragging blankets along. *One punch? Two?* I rocked and whimpered until exhaustion collapsed me, but I dozed for only a few minutes. Leslie's black eye haunted my sleep, jerking me awake, a cycle that repeated until breakfast. The final day of the retreat, with its twin lullabies of breath and bell, restored a measure of calm.

Back home, phone messages had to be returned, emails answered, postponed obligations met. The black eye and its implications receded.

Scouring powder swirled into foam as I scrubbed the kitchen sink. Water from the sprayer spiraled the bubbles down the drain, leaving behind a faint scent of bleach and the gleam of porcelain. Lost in daydreams, I turned off the faucet, patting it dry with a sponge. Someone—Wayne? Michael?—at some family gathering or another, had repeated an old story. That after Wayne, maybe in junior high at the time, had gone to bed, Dad went in to check on him. Startled awake, Wayne had yelled, "Don't kill me, Dad!"

I stiffened.

Not: Don't kill me, you mean-looking stranger who just broke into my room.

Don't kill me—Dad.

I tossed the sponge onto the counter and raced for the phone. "Wayne. Did Dad hit you?"

"Oh sure."

Leslie's matter-of-fact tone again. It floored me. "When? How often?"

"From the time I could first think, until I was a teenager." His voice level.

I felt faint... slumped into the nearest chair... held the phone to my ear without comprehension. Dad had assaulted Wayne and Leslie; he'd probably hit the rest of us, too.

We talked for an hour. Wayne must have shared other revelations, but after we hung up, our discussion vanished into the phone's dead air. It had taken decades to notice that memories of my childhood were sparse. Years to realize I was blocking out an unnamed truth. Would it take another lifetime before that truth could be assimilated? I was buffeted between a craving for information and an inability to absorb it.

My tenacity seemed otherworldly. An impersonal determination to face my personal reality, despite whatever pain might be included. And so, little by little, in fits and starts, I began to hear what my brothers said.

Michael said, "Dad swatted me so hard, it lifted me off the floor, propelled me forward."

After that call, I carried a load of laundry to the basement, my movements as mechanical as the washer's. I phoned him again a month later. "Do you remember what you said last month?"

"Yeah. Dad hit me so hard it lifted me off the floor." He told me three more times, in three different phone calls, before it sank in how hard that swat was.

Wayne said, "He threw Leslie against a wall."

After that call, I started on dinner. *Did he see it happen?* Stuck salmon fillets into the oven. *Did he say she fell?* Chopped lettuce, cucumber for salad. Mistook the ketchup for vinaigrette. The stove timer beeped. *Was he afraid?* Beeped again. I pulled burnt fish from the oven and called Wayne back. "Did you tell me Dad slammed Leslie into a wall?"

Michael said, "I was seven, scared of a bully at school. Dad threw me onto the sidewalk. Ordered me to go fight."

After that call, I gathered up garden tools, slipped on gloves, and set about my yard work. While plucking weeds with a trowel, I stabbed at a dandelion until it shredded. I called Michael back. "What did you mean—he threw you onto the sidewalk?"

Wayne said, "He whipped me with a razor strap. It was in our garage on Alan Road. My therapist said he should have gone to jail."

"How did it affect your life?" A safe question. Formality distanced me from mental movies: Dad wielding a strap like a plantation overseer, Dad pacing across a prison yard.

Wayne didn't seem to mind my therapeutic tone. "I isolate. I'm afraid of relationships. I don't want to get hit anymore."

He isolated. The description fit all of us. My brothers and sisters seldom spoke with one another. Marked holidays with friends instead of family. Phone messages went unheeded or unheard. We moved without providing new addresses. Nieces and nephews knew aunts and uncles only by name. Three of my siblings were married; I had skipped their weddings. They had not attended mine. I hadn't expected it.

My shoulders slumped under the weight of grief so dense it robbed me of tears. I did not remember Dad hitting me, but the threat of his violence held me hostage, even after his death. I felt oppressed and powerless. And yet, eventually, relieved to find out what kind of environment had forged my adult self. Disparate elements fell into place:

Night terrors. I had a recurring dream that a demon was coming to kill me. My siblings' disclosures made it clear the monster was Dad.

Men. I avoided tall men. Had never dated any man whose build resembled my father's muscular six-foot frame.

Headaches. A doctor labeled them migraines. Another blamed allergies. A feng shui master cited the wires under my bed. Low blood sugar. Barometric pressure. Tension. Of course, tension. Isn't that what you'd feel if your father was coming to kill you?

I remembered none of the nightmares my siblings had described, but their recollections revealed the painful truth that was lost to my amnesia. Once my life made sense, the forces that had compelled me to excavate my past evaporated. I stopped questioning Michael and Wayne. I felt at peace.

I snapped the laptop shut and set it on the floor. An email had led to a blog post which led to a website which led to a purchase. My eyes were glazed. I rested on the bed, let the memory foam mattress support my weary tailbone. *A razor strap? On Alan Road?*

When I was in grade school, a razor strap had hung on a hook beside the front door of our house on East 15th Street—Des Moines. After Dad and Mama divorced, Dad moved into an apartment by himself. From there, children and new wife in tow, to another house in Des Moines. From there to Altadena, California. To Voluntario Street in Santa Barbara. And then to Alan Road. Six houses. Five U-Hauls. Half a continent. Half a century. Dad held onto his fucking strap.

A breeze from the ceiling fan raised the hairs on my bare arms. My throat closed. Cicadas buzzed outside the window, and if I'd inclined my head in their direction, my body could have shaken off this final blow. Instead, face turned to the ceiling, I leaned back on my hands and moaned. Guttural. Primitive.

My subconscious shook loose one clear memory.

After school, I slunk home, trying to elude the snarling German shepherds that ran loose through our neighborhood. One more block to safety, half a block, the driveway, and finally, our brick sidewalk. I darted up the front steps. After the screen door slapped closed behind me, I turned to check for the dogs again, leaning into the porch screen mesh. It smelled metallic and dusty, and it pressed a grid into my forehead, to be admired later in the bathroom mirror. A board groaned as I crossed the porch. I bounced on it, then reached for the door into the house. The razor strap was draped over a hook beside the jamb. Too thick for its ends to meet, it hung in a stiff loop. The brown leather was worn to a sheen. I pretended it wasn't there, but my knees got fluttery and threatened to buckle. My stomach sickened, the way it did every morning after breakfast. I squeezed hard to keep from wetting my pants.

Fifty years later I shrieked at the ceiling fan. "Asshole! What kind of sadist—?" It wasn't enough to hit us. He had to display the weapon. Show it off. That's what I walked into every day?

I did not remember getting hit with the strap. Did not remember witnessing my siblings getting hit. I no longer needed to. One clear memory shook loose the declaration I hadn't yet expressed, in spite of all my questioning and all the resulting answers: Dad abused his children. Abused me.

How could I put *Dad* and *abuse* into the same sentence? How could I set them down side by side? It was an obscene juxtaposition. Sometimes, after the realization, I was too weary to lift a skillet or push a dust mop, the sadness like a straightjacket. In between, I was furious with my mother and my stepmother for not protecting us. And then, I was afraid of getting into trouble for telling. Worried that Dad's friends would accuse me of betraying him. But there was no disputing the black eye, the razor strap, the slam of a child's body against concrete. Dad. Abuse. One sentence.

Wayne confided, "I'm afraid I'm like him."

By the time he said it, that particular fear had already crossed into certainty for me.

My first husband and I were guardians of my nephew, Anthony. When he was eight, challenging, testing, I spanked him. That's what I called it.

I grabbed his wrist and dragged him to the basement, where I pounded his backside with a brush designed for washing cars. The thwack of every strike bounced off the cement walls. It was the only sound, because he refused to cry. He protected his bottom with his free hand. Even as he twisted away from the blows, he glared at me. He tried to yank his arm out of my grasp, but I squeezed it tighter and hit that kid with all my strength.

When he was fifteen, me a single mom and him spending the night with a buddy, I woke up at three a.m. Those whippings replayed in an endless loop. I screamed at the memory, stuffing the blanket in my mouth so the neighbors wouldn't call the police. In the morning, at the kitchen sink, the flashbacks returned, and I collapsed onto the floor. As hard as I tried to twist my mind away from it, I could not escape the assault. The dank air of the basement, the thwack of the brush, Anthony's arm crushed inside my fist.

So, when he returned home from the sleepover, I sat him down at the kitchen table. "I owe you an apology."

He said, "Huh?"

It must have thrown him for a loop. A willful teenager, he was used to me demanding an apology instead of offering one.

"You were in third grade... I shouldn't have whipped you... it was wrong."

He said, "What?" He leaned toward me, his gaze piercing the space between us.

"You didn't deserve to be hit. Ever. I was wrong. I'm sorry."

His hands, bigger than mine, rested on the table in front of him.

"When you have kids, I don't want you to think it's all right to hit them. It's not."

"Okay." Stoicism veiled his feelings, but his eyes continued to bore into mine.

Anthony had inherited a legacy of violence. Could one mea culpa cancel out its effects? Perhaps he'd already learned cruelty from me the way I'd learned it from Dad.

My father intrudes on my thinking, until I doubt my brain has ever produced an original idea. If I recite a joke with pitch-perfect timing, it's his timing, not mine. His opinions attach themselves to the items tossed into my grocery cart. If you're behind me in line, and we've been trading stories like we've known each other since kindergarten, you're talking to my father. One of Dad's colleagues chuckles when I peer at her over my reading glasses. "God, you look just like Bill." I take it as a compliment. He was an author before me, as well as a teacher, and one of his students says of my writing, "The apple doesn't fall too far from the tree." Which one of us is the apple, which one the tree?

On retreat, after Matthew's dharma talk, I met with him in a private session. "All these years, all the teachings you've shared... I thought it was you, lecturing me. But it was my own voice trying to wake myself up."

Acceptance. It sounds so gentle; you foolishly imagine you might try it. As if you could choose. You don't choose. You plummet into acceptance, because the floor has collapsed beneath your feet. Surrender to the fact of razor strap; from there surrender to shock; from there to rage, to grief, to relief, and back to grief. Always back to grief. To the bruised faces of children across the planet, the faces of the fathers who bruised them and the mothers who turned away. And when you crash into what you presume is the very sub-basement of surrender, a sinkhole opens and swallows you. Surrender to that.

There's no hitting the bottom of acceptance, only a rush of irrational affection for all the voices in your life. They are your own.

At my grandmother's, we always put away the toys when we finished playing, probably drawn to the kitchen by the scent of pumpkin pie fresh from the oven. I carried the dollhouse back to the attic, holding it in both hands, even though it was light enough to balance in one, keeping it level to prevent the furniture from sliding into chaos. Although my sister might play with it before my next visit, and I might need to return the bed to its rightful spot under the window, I always found the dollhouse tucked into a corner of the attic, near the tea set and the Lincoln logs. The brick chimney always rose from the peak of the roof. Pristine, impotent, because the dollhouse had no fireplace. There are advantages to such an arrangement. No ashes to cart away. No danger of stray embers popping onto a carpet. And yet... no hypnotic flicker. No heat. No crackle.

Part IV

Oneness Makes Strange Bedfellows:
Losing My Self

Even though I'm not Catholic, I was watching television, waiting for white smoke to billow from the Sistine Chapel's chimney.

As Pope Francis stepped onto the balcony, my tears welled, even though...

He smiled easily. He joked a bit, his voice soft and small against the storms awaiting him. One old man, shouldering the hopes of a billion people. When he asked us to pray for him, I closed my eyes along with the faithful crowded into St. Peter's Square, even though...

Thich Nhat Hahn said, "Call me by my true names."

For now, before my opinions reclaim my attention, call me catholic.

Clear Comprehension without Delusion

The camera zoomed in on a pathologist's rubber-gloved hands as he sliced through a torso. A thin line of maroon trailed the scalpel. He peeled back the skin, thick and gray, like a roll of attic insulation.

Matthew had assigned our sangha to watch a video that showed a series of autopsies. The purpose: to dislodge attachment to the body as something special, and help us to gain, in the words of the Buddha, "clear comprehension without delusion" that there was no self in said body. Other than the gore, it was familiar territory.

Mystics of every persuasion, Hindu and Christian as well as Buddhist, taught that life was selfless. The words were repeated in books and dharma talks—I knew what they meant. It seemed clear enough that, whenever I spaced out for twenty minutes, a force other than me was driving the car, washing the dishes, or sweeping the patio.

So, okay. No self in the body. I got it.

I downloaded the video from the Internet. My first reaction was nausea. While describing the procedure as though reciting a grocery list, the pathologist lifted unrecognizable, blood-soaked organs from inside the body of a man and placed them into stainless steel bowls. He was discussing a diseased liver when the download froze and then jumped to an entirely different corpse, female. Her/its naked midsection filled the computer screen. As the grainy footage flickered, tension contorted my face. My lips puckered. The cords in my neck tightened.

The pathologist sliced across the rib cage, lifted the dense layer of skin, breasts and all, and laid it over the head.

I gagged, lightheaded.

Breasts were the core of womanhood, the heart of femininity, the source of primal angst. Throughout my adult life they'd triggered rage when they were gawked at and anguish when they went unnoticed. One pierce of a scalpel obliterated my personal connection to femaleness. Jesus, breasts were only extra padding on a sheet of insulation.

The download skipped around. A policeman discussing the importance of forensics to a high-profile murder case. A medical student explaining why she wanted to pursue pathology. Then the playback froze again.

Centered in the frame, a close-up of a chest and stomach cavity. No blood or fat to obscure the view. The organs packed neatly into place. Straight from the factory. Intestines like steel tubing, glinting with mechanical efficiency. If the pathologist had prodded with his scalpel, it would have clinked.

I wasn't grossed out anymore. I was stunned.

It was the view under the hood of a racecar. Computer circuitry. The workings of a robot.

That's what I am? A machine programmed to believe it's a person?

My mind went blank. I shut down the computer and went to bed.

Early in the morning, I pad barefoot through the house; our hardwood floors squeak with every step. In the kitchen, sticking a bowl of oatmeal into the microwave, I glimpse my reflection in the glass door. My skin looks metallic, my eyes like black marbles, my expression soulless.

A robot.

My knees buckle. Groaning, I collapse in slow motion, end up bent over with my head on the counter. Loose grains of sugar dig into my forearms. I can't stand up. What am I feeling? Something too immense to be corralled by words. Too physical to be depicted by language. Ben finds me sinking toward the floor. I manage to sputter, "Matt. Autopsy video. No self." I can't catch my breath. A meditation teacher himself, Ben doesn't seem to need more explanation, lifts me gently to my feet, "Come on, sweetheart, let's sit on the bench." He sits beside me, wraps me in his arms, pats my hand, kisses my head, rocks me. None of it makes sense. He's a robot, too. His words merely a track on a CD playing inside his skull. I am not comforted, but allow the comforting to continue.

My sobbing abates. Calm settles into my body, but peace eludes me.

"Do you want to talk about it?" he asks.

"I don't know what to say."

He nods. The microwave dings.

Muscle memory propels me through daily obligations. Habit creates a pretense of normality, while my gut remains bilious, a constant reminder that life has taken a turn toward science fiction. I meet a friend for coffee, my usual chattiness stifled. She fills in the blank spaces with news about grandchildren and reads her latest poem to me. Does she know she's a machine? I feel heartsick for her. If she finds out, how will she go on? How will I? And if life proves too overwhelming to go on, I won't even be the author of the decision to end it.

Our yoga teacher challenges us with backbend, a pose more advanced than we're used to. I dread this part of class. I am not excited about attempting poses that, if performed improperly, will result in broken bones or broken pride. Afterward, as usual, she grins. "Wasn't that fun?" she asks. I'm shocked, because my body responds yes, definitely. It's wandered into a pleasure cloud that's floating around the studio. The enjoyment is surreal and provokes melancholy, as though my closest friend has moved away.

Our book group facilitator interrupts a participant's personal reflection to tell a joke. He does this every week, and every week I'm annoyed. This time, the reaction is short-circuited. His banter and my exasperation are both familiar tracks that our CDs repeat. Neither of us is responsible for the music or the dance. We're in it together, sounding the occasional sour note, stepping on each other's toes, driven by habits worn into mind and flesh. Whole-body muscle memory.

Programming, then, was the "force other than me" that pointed the car toward home whenever I lapsed into daydreaming. Pre-autopsy-video, I'd mistakenly assumed responsibility for the activity that took place between those gaps in alertness. Post-autopsy-video, I realized there was no me to be other than. But why did it...? How could that...? What should I...? Rationality was too depleted by shock to power questions into full existence. They looped back upon themselves, with nothing at the core. The program itself created all the queries. It wrote every poem. And by grace, it uploaded the message there's no self in the body.

No Longer Mother

The tumor in Mother's breast brought our five-year estrangement to an end. I moved back home to care for her.

"What made you decide to come?" she asked, days before morphine suppressed her language skills.

"I didn't want you to die while we weren't speaking."

Cancer had shrunk her sweater-girl figure to a speck in her king-sized bed. Magazines she could no longer read lay scattered around her. Her sketchpad topped a stack of books on the floor. Brass figurines crowded her nightstand: Lord Ganesha on his throne, Shiva and Shakti intertwined, and Buddha touching the earth. Her earrings hung from a corkboard leaning behind them. Next to it, a bottle of Chanel No. 5.

When a hospital bed replaced Mother's California king, she looked exposed and temporary, lying in the center of a stripped-down cell.

She liked to relax in a rocking chair in the living room, until fatigue overpowered even that small pleasure.

I helped her return to bed, sliding backward in my sock feet as she shuffled forward facing me. She held my hands like a baby learning to walk. A moan, buried deep in her throat, accentuated the brushing of her feet across the floor. Our progress was erratic, our pace languid.

We stopped to rest, alone in the house and toe-to-toe in the grief-shrouded hallway.

I searched her Natalie Wood eyes for the woman who'd waited up for teenaged me to come home from dates. For the woman who'd lived in swashes of color: pink lipstick, turquoise jewelry, violet dresses. For the woman who'd painted our dining room red.

She looked right back. Unflinching attention replaced the morphine stare. I was startled for a beat. And then I leaned toward her, careful to maintain our fragile balance, yet longing to close the space between us. Remnants of our past—harsh words and good intentions—flew away on our mingled breath. Her gaze drew me in, cradled me halfway between this world and the next.

No longer daughter.

No longer Mother.

Men wearing black suits wheeled her out of the house, through the living room where my family gathered, past the rocking chair where Dad slumped, weeping.

I curled up in the hospital bed, tucking her blankets under my chin. Eternity sang me to sleep, and Chanel No. 5 wafted through my dreams.

Call to Prayer

"I need Thee, oh I need Thee." A quartet at the front of the sanctuary led the congregation through the hymn. The singers' eyes were closed; the a cappella chords seemed to lift them to a plane where sight was irrelevant.

From my pew, I mumbled the lyrics in a suggestion of song, more thought than utterance. "Every hour I need Thee."

Regulars who occupied the side section, closest to the drums and organ, were on their feet, their arms raised like the branches of pear trees in spring. Ahead of me, in the center section, others danced in place. Step. Clap-step. Step. Clap-step.

The quartet's voices faded as the performers turned away from us to face the altar. As if their movements had been choreographed, they bowed their heads and reached for each other's hands.

"Oh bless me now, my Savior." They swayed in unison, their harmonies barely audible.

I nodded in time with the music. "I come to Thee."

Pastor Howard claimed his position behind the sacred desk. His white robe, accented by two gold stripes that ran from shoulder to hem, hung in folds around him. He rested his hands on the Bible. "Is there anyone here who needs to come to Him now?"

A white-haired deacon lumbered down the aisle past my pew to join the soloists at the altar.

Pastor held his hand out in invitation. His gaze pinpointed a family to my left. "Do you need a special prayer today?" Or maybe the question was directed at me. His voice offered respite. "I need Thee," he sang.

Others rose to make the pilgrimage. Ancient ladies—bent and heavy—lumbered down the carpeted aisle. A little boy clutched the hand of his grandfather. Church matrons marched, their spines ramrod straight. All of them, both the slow-paced and the quick, a great migration moving inexorably toward water.

What made them certain their thirst would be quenched?

The answer eluded me, in spite of the past five years, Sunday mornings spent on the fourth pew from the front, aisle seat, just behind Sister Rose. Every Sunday after service, I quizzed Pastor Howard about a passage in his message. And every Sunday he laughed. "Thank you for being here. You're such a blessing."

"But why?"

He put his hands on my shoulders. His voice softened; I had to concentrate to hear him. "Just showing up," he said, "you bless everyone around you." He laughed again. Full-throated devotion of Baptist service gave voice to my spirit and a swing to my hips, until, perhaps, I was worshiping. Although I didn't know what resided at the receiving end of that adoration, it felt natural to bow down before the miracle (God?) that set my left foot in front of my right, step after step, day after day.

Natural? Yes. Enough? No.

At silent retreats, you worship an unsentimental search for truth. You worship words like investigation and nonduality. Your teacher, Matt, exhorts you to examine your mind, you and your fellow seekers engrossed in his dharma talk. How many dharma talks is this? How many retreats? His voice grows soft at the precise moment someone coughs—drowning out the essential phrase that would have transformed the nature of your existence. You are rigid, focused, a zebra scanning the breeze for the scent of lion. Your life depends on this. Matt concludes the talk with a homework assignment. For the next three hours, you're supposed to trace each thought back to its beginning. When you try to rise, your knees buckle. Your shoulders ache, your back too, but you limp along the hiking trails that crisscross the grounds of the the retreat center. Staring at your thoughts. And when you witness the birth of one of your less profound reflections—*there's never enough salad at dinner*—things go impossibly quiet. You stiffen. You hold your breath. You have stumbled upon the place prior to. Wandered right into the source. You're not thinking it; you're knowing it. But then it's gone, and you have to get it back. You have to. So you drag yourself back to the meditation hall and sit. Again.

"Please rise. Let us pray."

Pastor Howard's instruction brought me to my feet. I bowed my head.

"Heavenly Father, we thank You for giving us another day to gather in Your name."

I stuck my toe into the aisle, then gave way for a slender auntie—regal in a wide-brimmed orange hat that matched her suit and pumps—who was striding to the front. Her wake carried me to the altar. I approached two matrons among the assembled group, reached out until my fingers grazed theirs. They opened a space for me, each squeezing my hand in welcome. I squeezed back.

We inched closer and closer together until our arms

touched. Our sweaty palms stuck together. As they rocked side to side with the beat, my feet picked up the rhythm. The woman on my right slipped away, placing my hand into someone else's. Beefy and rough, it swallowed mine.

"We lift up Sister Johnson," Pastor said, "who's in the hospital recovering from heart surgery."

"Yes, Lord," a voice from the choir loft responded.

"We pray for Brother Robinson, still looking for a job, amen."

"Well, well." A rumble in front of me.

"We lift up Mother Crockett who had a stroke last week. And the Sims family—their son William shot on Friday. And we pray, Lord, that you keep our young men safe."

"Hallelujah." A wail from the left.

"And we lift up..."

Chords from the piano ran though the prayer, like a creek gurgling in the distance. An old woman whimpered. A baby wailed. The man next to me danced in the opposite direction, and we collided. He raised his arms with a "Help me, Jesus," lifting mine, too.

Pastor's prayer rolled over us. "Lord, we thank you for bringing us through tragedies this week. Thank you for the power of the Holy Ghost."

Head still bowed, I peeked. On my right, brown shoes sticking out from under cuffed trousers. To the left, purple stilettos, pink toes. Red patent Mary Janes, white ruffled anklets. In front, the hems of skirts swishing—

"... every hour, Lord!" Pastor spread his arms, as if he were parting the Red Sea. White sleeves billowed. Gold stripes flashed. Sweat glistened on his forehead. He looked toward heaven with closed eyes.

I squeezed mine shut again.

The piano matched the reverend's voice, decibel for decibel. A drum punctuated his appeals. Vibrations shook the floor, trembled through my feet, and shuddered up my spine. Praise was popping all around.

And yet... an elemental stillness crept into the foreground of my awareness. There at the core of my breath, on the cusp of every drumbeat and the apex of every toe tap. There in the pause before a sway to the left turned into a sway to the right. A silence prior to the absence of sound. Here?

Here. Without investigation. Without Matthew. No search. Only song.

The pastor's baritone slid down from thunder to lullaby. "Thank you, God, for waking us up this morning. Let the people of the church say amen."

"Amen."

I staggered back down the aisle. My temples pulsed. Legs trembled. A spasm shook my arm. Reclaiming my spot, I clutched the back of the pew to steady myself.

The choir director stepped forward, turned to face the chorus, and signaled with a nod of her head. The singers inhaled, set flight to another hymn. "I come to the garden alone..."

The gentle tune washed over me. My muscles relaxed. Step. Clap-step. Step. Clap-step. "While the dew is still on the roses..." I sang out my praise to the source.

Blurred Edges

My husband and I hopped out of the car, excited to explore a stand of aspens, trees that outdoorsy friends had called magical. Because one root system connected the plants, each colony was a single organism. It gave the appearance of many where there was only one.

My pace slowed as I approached the grove; Ben wandered off ahead. White trunks, slender enough to embrace, flanked me. I leaned back and craned my neck for a view of the canopy. Round leaves quaked in the mountain breeze, pinpoints of green strobing against the blue sky.

Careful to avoid trampling ankle-high sprouts, I crept toward the center. As the edge of the stand disappeared, the roar of traffic diminished, and the faint tap of a woodpecker replaced my internal chatter. My sense of direction fell away, then my sense of me. Without others nearby for comparison, I was no longer Democrat or Republican, introvert or extrovert, clever or dull. Was my outfit stylish? My hair combed? In the absence of someone to call it, did I have a name? My palms were dusted with white powder rubbed from the aspen trunks. Rocked by the mountain breeze, I was an anonymous sapling springing from the common root.

We'd flown to Colorado so Ben could officiate at a wedding

in Durango. The groom put us up in a house that belonged to friends—photographers vacationing overseas. The couple had built their home at the end of a winding dirt road on the outskirts of town. Designed it with expansive windows in every room, sweeps of glass that commanded views of high desert. Off the kitchen, they'd added a deck and installed bird feeders, where hummingbirds sipped nectar alongside human coffee drinkers. A garden beyond that, fenced in for protection from deer. Beyond that, the plateaus gave way to the San Juan Mountains.

At first I savored those views, but by the third day, little irritations filtered into my chitchat. "With all their money," I said to Ben, "you'd think they could afford curtains."

No matter where I planted myself, the great outdoors threatened to devour me. I wanted solid walls, with nature kept at bay.

I thought the bathroom offered sanctuary, but noticed a window near the ceiling, facing the toilet. A blue jay perched on the sill.

I stormed into the bedroom where Ben was napping. "This house has boundary issues."

A closet served as my dressing room—not a walk-in, but a storage space lined with shelves. In there among the sheets, I cracked my elbow and stubbed my toes whenever I squeezed into my jeans.

"What are you doing?" Ben asked.

"Not stripping down in front of that." I pointed to the bedroom's floor-to-ceiling window and the walkway on the other side of it, which wrapped around the house.

"There's nobody out there."

"It's looking at me."

"What is?"

"Colorado."

I was lost in it. I longed to reclaim my significance.

All that glass, but not a single mirror big enough to help me tilt my wide-brimmed hat to an appropriately jaunty angle. I searched through our luggage for something more useful than my compact.

A photograph of a Buddhist monk in Myanmar hung over the bed, his peaceful eyes gazing into the camera lens. My face was superimposed on his, reflected in the glass. It caught me off guard. I turned away. A portrait of a nun hung near the door. Our features blurred into a single countenance. When I softened my focus, her pale pink robes hung from my shoulders, and my straw hat covered her head. Next to hers, a photo of saffron-robed boys trooping across the grounds of a monastery. Their skin golden, their heads shaved. Two of them were giggling. And I appeared among them, as a ghostly visage floating overhead.

My reflected faces all looked like Mama Catherine's, in a photo taken when I was four. We were standing side by side, framed by the back doorway of our house in Ottumwa. Mama's arms were crossed, her expression stoic. She stared out beyond the camera, suspended above the moment.

Where did I begin or end? Born in Ottumwa, living in Kansas City, standing in Durango, peering at myself in Mandalay.

Back home, during a meeting, my visual perception shifted. As the group settled into meditation, our edges blurred. The circle of individuals coalesced into a single organism. Chests rose and fell on a common breath. A stand of aspens shivering in a mountain breeze.

Palin Power:
On Discovering the Emptiness of Knowledge

2oo8. On the first night of the Democratic convention, I clicked out of Politico.com, MSNBC.com, and NYTimes.com, turned off the radio's political analyst, and raced to the den to catch public television's coverage. I'd been a Yellow Dog Democrat since the autumn we turned playground four-square into a political forum: pitypat if you said you were for Kennedy, but if you said Nixon, we got you out right away. (Years later John Dean vindicated my early instincts.)

The wife of our nominee—African-American Senator Barack Obama—headlined opening night. The senator personified my party's big tent ideals, but Michelle Obama... she was something else altogether. She was somebody like me. Hips like mine, almond-shaped eyes like mine, hair straightened with the chemicals that had smoothed my tresses back when I was her age, the acrid odor easily summoned in spite of the intervening years. Her presence on that stage filled me with pride and righteousness. It was personal.

As the convention unfolded over the week, a procession of elected officials lauded the vision of the Democrats and poked fun at the Republicans. I nodded in agreement when they recounted the failures of the current GOP administration. I yelled my approval at their proposals for whipping our government back into shape. Conventioneers, draped in lanyards bearing their credentials, hooted and stabbed the air with placards. We were Democrats, and we knew what the country needed, by God. I remained in front of the television from opening gavel to grand finale, when nominee Obama described the election as a defining moment.

The Republicans gathered the following week. I tuned in to hear what the other side was plotting. When their politicians poked fun at the Democrats, my back stiffened. Their personal attacks went too far. I shook my head as they enumerated the mistakes (or so they called them) of previous Democratic administrations. They claimed those who fell for wrong-headed left-wing propaganda and liberal media bias were either gullible or stupid. What? We Dems possessed well-researched facts; those Republicans held misguided opinions. I jeered at their proposals, while conventioneers, draped in lanyards bearing their credentials, hooted and stabbed the air with placards.

Why did they look so sure of themselves? So... familiar? It didn't make sense. The conviction I'd felt as a liberal was shining through conservative eyes. My left-wing self-assurance echoed in the cheers of a right-wing mob. *My* conviction. *My* self-assurance. How could they be expressing my zeal? Was it possible I felt theirs?

People I'd known to be Wild-Eyed Fanatics were crystallizing into People Like Me.

As conservative politicians took to the stage and denounced my left-wing party, I was dumbfounded. But not because of their beliefs. I was dumbfounded because of mine. Beliefs—that's all I had. Not knowledge. Beliefs.

Republicans knew we were wrong in exactly the same way I knew we were right.

They railed against crime. I understood. After all, I knew it was no big deal to leave my front door unlocked, in the same way my neighbor knew to triple-bolt hers.

They railed against taxes. I got it. After all, I knew it was fair that everybody pay them, in the same way my accountant knew I should pay nothing.

The cameras panned the audience again.

The members of the Texas delegation sported identical red plaid shirts and white cowboy hats. I waited for my habitual scorn to list their deficiencies, waited for my disdain to restore balance to the world. Waited in vain, because I couldn't say with certainty the Lone Star State even existed. You'd never see its familiar shape, peer out of an airplane as long or often as you want. Texas was a belief.

Disoriented, I wrapped up in a throw and sank back into the couch. A massage of my temples provided no relief. The political fire in my belly sputtered out. There would be no yard signs, buttons, or tee shirts. They don't make bumper stickers for Republi-Crats.

A fresh round of applause from the convention floor. A speaker introduced the candidate for the vice presidency: Sarah Palin. Conservative. Charismatic. Controversial. The political blogosphere rumored she supported a party that advocated Alaskan secession from the US.

"Ladies and gentleman, the next vice president of the United States."

My knees weakened. My palms sweated. Butterflies were fluttering. I wanted to pace, then fought back an urge to rush to the nearest restroom. Symptoms of... stage fright?

Stage fright.

But why me?

"Sarah Palin." She strode from behind the curtains. The hall erupted in a roaring, foot-stomping ovation, which whiplashed me from *Get out of here!* to *I'm about to obliterate my opponents.*

She click-clacked across the stage, waving, grinning, and throwing kisses.

I felt my feet encased in her stiletto peep-toe pumps, and with each step she advanced, the floor pounded against my soles.

Thousands of adoring fans chanted, "Sarah, Sarah, Sarah."

They may as well have shouted, "Dawn, Dawn, Dawn."

I didn't understand my visceral response to her. It scared me, but I couldn't make it stop. Sarah Palin was pushing me off a cliff.

She took her place at the lectern.

My confidence swelled as she read her speech; she and I had prepared for this big moment. She—I—did not step on our applause lines. She delivered our zingers with the timing of Johnny Carson.

Her final "God bless America" set off another wave of thunder from the floor, where new signs had appeared: "Palin Power," "Hockey Moms 4 Palin." The presidential candidate joined her on the stage. The crowd roared. The ceiling parted. The balloons dropped. My chest swelled with pride. *You go, girl. Work that crowd.*

She winked into the camera. At me.

I plummeted into free fall—became this woman who I wanted to dismiss, adored this woman with whom I felt no kinship. She was no Michelle Obama. My adoration transcended pride and righteousness. The physical space between Sarah Palin and me imploded, as a singular humanity displaced the conceit there had ever been two of us.

The Buddha said, "In the seeing, just the seen." There she stood, seen, she and her Republicans, undistorted by the stories my so-called knowledge had composed. My entire store of information turned out to be a collection of beliefs, which I'd mislabeled facts. The whole idea of *knowing* fell apart.

The campaign lurched forward, an exercise in democracy equally meaty for political analysts and gossipmongers—God, certainty, and outrage on both sides of every issue. When companions opined about the candidates, I kept silent. No longer saw the GOP as the party of evildoers, no longer viewed the Democrats as white knights. My interest in politics, whether environmental, feminist, or social, became less frantic. I relaxed. The election was a novel—a darn good one, but I could put it down any time.

2012. The presidential race was a political junkie's dream come true. A dead heat.

The caller on my cell identified herself as a volunteer for the Democratic Party. "Will you be voting?"

"You bet. Never miss an election."

"We need your help to get the president re-elected."

Her sales pitch would normally have precipitated my goodbye, but I'd always aspired to work on a political campaign, even though I'd never possessed the nerve to act on the aspiration. It was easier, now in my sixties, to consider her request as opportunity, rather than annoyance. "Like what?"

"Let's sit down over coffee."

"Okay. Next week is good."

We met for breakfast. She wore a blue Obama baseball cap and a white Obama sweatshirt. An Obama tote bag hung from one shoulder, spilling over with papers, bunting, and clipboards. She spread leaflets and pencils on our table before handing me a form.

"Check the things you'd be willing to do."

I retrieved my glasses from my purse. Let's see. Phone

bank? Call my fellow Democrats and get an earful about the sinister motives of Republicans? No, thanks.

Knock on doors to convince others to vote Democratic? Impossible. Republican opinions were just as valid as mine.

Surely there was something... less... evangelical.

Data entry? Boring.

Voter registration? Yes. That I could do.

She outlined the details, and then raised a Styrofoam cup to her lips. "Girl, after the mess the Republicans got us into..."

I pushed my glasses to the top of my head.

"... disaster if they win."

I munched on a bagel, imagined her reading to the grandchildren she'd mentioned earlier, rather than holding forth on the subject that now tightened the muscles in her neck.

"... back to the bad old days. You know what's at stake." Her voice grew shrill to compete with an espresso machine that shrieked in the background.

Voter registration was anti-climactic. I criss-crossed parking lots, intercepting shoppers as they emerged from big-box stores. Set up shop in deserted student unions at community colleges. Loitered in a high school cafeteria, as disinterested teenagers wolfed down pizza. The isolation heightened the limbo I inhabited: a political landscape with no bogeyman to demonize, no hero to lionize, and no dogma to advertise.

On the evening of the first presidential debate, I clicked out of my gardening website, meandered to the kitchen where I stared into the fridge, hoping dinner would materialize, and then wandered into the den to turn on the television.

It was the president's wedding anniversary. He directed his opening remarks to the First Lady, who watched from the front row. "I promise we won't be spending our next anniversary in front of fifty million people." A half-smile flashed across his face. During the debate, he seldom made eye contact with the camera, and by extension, us—his supporters. His brow was furrowed, his face deeply lined. His hair had grayed over the past four years.

His opponent was energized. He was attentive to the president while waiting to speak. His eyes were bright when he looked into the camera. A businessman, a regular citizen, on stage arguing with POTUS. I puffed up with unexpected pride on his behalf.

I rooted for the president, but worried about him, too. Had he slept well the night before? Did he really want the job? Crises erupting all over the globe... what imminent war had he put on hold to show up for this verbal combat? I rooted for him, partly because I hated the thought of him going home afterward, on his anniversary, feeling like a failure.

And what about his opponent? He put so much into this campaign, dragged his family through a media circus. His look-alike sons out there on the trail for Dad. Assuring us he was just as corny as he came across on the stump. A guy sincerely clueless about his image... well, I found his goofiness irresistible. He believed in his solutions so strongly, you could tell he wasn't just responding to polls. He knew the country would elect him, because it just made sense, darn it. If he lost, he'd be devastated, sure, but bewildered, too. I hated to imagine him sliding into depression.

Which of them will I vote for? This Yellow Dog Democrat will blacken the circle beside the president's name, of course.

Which of them will better serve the country? Hmm. Don't believe I know.

Precious Moments

"Don't laugh; I want to stop at Precious Moments on the way home." My husband accelerated the Chevy to pass an SUV. We crossed the Arkansas border into Missouri, cruising north on Highway 71.

The odds that Ben was serious about the Precious Moments stop were equal to the odds I would sprout wings and fly out the car window. Which I would definitely attempt if it turned out he was in earnest. On previous trips along this route, he'd tormented me with an offer to visit the Precious Moments Park and Chapel, Mecca for those who collected the porcelain figurines.

Our running joke usually began about ten miles from the exit.

"Sweetheart." His voice dripped with the saccharine overload that made the collectibles famous. "I've been trying to find a way to express my love for you." Five miles out, he'd deliver the punch line. "Let's renew our vows in the Precious Moments Chapel."

I would allude to hell freezing over and feign finger-down-throat gagging. "You sure?" he'd say. "Last chance."

This time, his tone sounded genuine. If I held my breath, maybe he'd forget the impulse.

He didn't. "I'm curious about how that whole development's changed in the last twenty years."

Doomed. He'd said the magic word: curious. I loved his curiosity. Because of it we'd ended up parked in a field of sunflowers or surrounded by locomotives in a train yard at midnight, or best of all, questioned by an armed guard when we ventured too close to an isolated power plant. My husband's inquisitive brain transformed our daily errands into exploits worthy of Bilbo Baggins.

I accepted my Precious Moments fate. It might be fun. We would share sarcastic jokes and exchange sidelong glances. I sharpened my razor wit in preparation.

"But no teasing," he added. "Let me look around without any flak."

What? How was I supposed to get through it without flak?

He pulled into a parking space. It was 102 degrees with 112 percent humidity. The weather alone brought out my sarcasm, yet he'd asked me to be good. I steeled myself to the challenge.

An imposing fountain blocked our entrance to the Visitors Center. Four concrete Precious Moments figures (PMs) and an equal number of frolicking geese encircled a trout as tall as me, which was dancing upright on its tail. Streams of water arced from the smiling beaks of the geese over to the trout, which spat a jet straight into the air. The PMs wore halos, or possibly dinner plates.

I hurried past, fearful a closer study of the tableau would force me to ignore Ben's request for harmony.

Having cleared the first hurdle, I followed hubby into the Visitors' Center. I gasped. Floor-to-ceiling display shelves lined the walls. Ten thousand tear-shaped black eyes stared at me from otherwise featureless beige faces, framed by wavy taupe hair. In this Aryan utopia, even the non-white children looked white. Those I took to be Asian bore identical faces, spray painted lemon yellow with straight black hair. African Americans sprayed tan, with caps of black curls. Hordes of Stepford children frozen into blissed-out poses. They watered tulips, kissed cardinals, rode scooters, danced under umbrellas, splashed in puddles.

A saleswoman approached us. "Hi. Welcome to Precious Moments. Been here before?"

I tensed up, scowled, then softened my expression, remembering my pledge.

My husband, who would say howdy to a fence post, shook her outstretched hand. "Well, I was here about twenty years ago. Came by today to see what's changed."

"You're in luck. Let me show you Hallelujah Square. It's a Chapel exclusive."

Hallelujah Square. Probably where they'll sacrifice me and pluck out my—."

"Great. Thanks." Ben took my clammy hand in his and followed the clerk to a display table piled high with gift boxes.

She pointed to a figurine in front of the boxes. A PM, holding a paintbrush, perched atop a stepladder. The little guy was painting a mural, which depicted other PMs.

Using the sides of her hands, the clerk turned the figurine so that we could see the back of it. "This shipment is all signed and numbered. But what's interesting is that these on the table were mislabeled. You see it's titled *Disney Suite*, when clearly it's *Hallelujah Square*. These will be worth a lot of money to collectors."

"Wow," Ben said. "What's Hallelujah Square?"

"Oh. The real one is out in the chapel. You've got to see that."

Off we went. I knew one thing about the Precious Moments Chapel. The ceiling was modeled after the Sistine Chapel ceiling. Except, well, PMs instead of people.

Concrete angels lined the walkway that led to the chapel. Their bulbous heads balanced precariously on narrow sloping shoulders—no necks. Each cherub held a horn to his face. The effort indicated by their puffed cheeks produced only silence, since these little Gabriels had no mouths with which to blow their horns.

We passed through ornately carved oak doors and into the chapel. Long and narrow like a Renaissance cathedral, the shape of the room drew me in past the Bible scenes painted on the walls, toward the main attraction at the far end.

The "real" *Hallelujah Square* was a mural depicting a place by the same name: the entryway to Heaven. Bewinged and haloed pastel children milled around on a pathway that led to glowing mountain peaks in the distance. Other tots floated above them or knelt on clouds, strumming harps. A group in the foreground welcomed a new arrival, a little boy. He'd just ascended from his bedroom, where his PM family was still gathered around his deathbed.

If Heaven looks like this, please let me sin my way into the other place.

A plaque on the wall informed me that the boy entering Heaven was the artist's deceased son, Philip. The bedroom was his. The mural a memorial to his memory.

A pang of guilt shot through my chest. *Poor man... to have his baby die...*

More details. Philip had died at the age of thirty.
Thirty?

For a second I thought it odd, but only for a second. Our children remain our babies, no matter how old they are.

Fortunately, Ben's bladder shortened our visit to PM Heaven.

Preserved in a locked glass case like the Constitution, a framed document hung on the wall in the hallway. The biography of Sam Butcher, PM's founder/creator/artist. "Poor boy born during the depression... loved to draw... couldn't afford supplies."

I adjusted my glasses.

"...used rolls of paper retrieved from a factory dump near his house."

Oh dear, how sad. A lad in tatters scrounging through a trash heap for art supplies.

The artist summed up his PM vision with one phrase: called by God to paint Bible scenes in which all the characters had childlike faces.

Sarcastic Dawn would have pounced all over this. *This guy has no idea what God sounds like. Every whacko says he's called by God.*

But, actually, Sam was telling the truth. His Truth. Who am I to question it? After all, I have no idea how God sounds, either.

I wanted Sarcastic Dawn back. I liked her. She made me feel smart. The reflection in the glass revealed my color had drained, along with my skepticism. I was as pale as a PM.

Ben found me wilted against a wall. "What's wrong?"

"Let's just go home."

"You look like you lost your best friend."

"I did."

He waited.

"If God is responsible for everything, you know what that means?"

He shook his head.

"*Everything*—this horrifies me. *Everything* includes Precious Moments."

He pursed his lips, as if to consider the plausibility. "Hmmm. Good point." He nodded. "Hey, let's stop in the gift shop."

Clearly, he did not understand how depressing this was. I had just announced the apocalypse. We walked through the oak doors out into the sunlight. "No, Ben. I'm serious. Listen." I pointed frantically at the sky with both hands and then spread my arms outward in a gesture of inclusion. "If Oneness is all there is, that includes Precious Moments. If there is nothing other than All That Is, then that includes Precious Moments. If nothing— do you hear me, *nothing*—is excluded, then that includes Precious Moments."

He regarded me with a faint smile and glanced at his watch.

I had to remember his disinterest was also included.

He squeezed my hand. "Okay, no gift shop. I'm ready to go, too."

When he opened my car door for me, I stopped. Were his eyes twinkling? What was that sound? Was he humming?

I pointed my finger at his nose. "I'm warning you, buddy. Do not surprise me with a Precious Moment to commemorate this day."

Part V

A Question a Day Keeps the Answers Away:
Making Peace with Paradox

What am I doing awake at... four in the morning? Should be crashed for weeks after that workout at the Y. *It's fun to stay at the YMCA.* May as well meditate. Yeah, yellow will look great in the bathroom. Getting sleepy. Sleepy. Sneezy. Dopey. Sleazy? Don't move. Wow, my face relaxed. That's weird. Nobody gets a tense face. Tense shoulders, maybe. Pl-e-e-e-z, let me go back to sl-e-e-e-p. Cardinal singing. Wonder how to tell a mocking bird from the bird it's mocking. *I said young man—*

The dreamed one dreams of insomnia.

Paradise

I meditated alone on a ridge two hundred feet above a river, with only my ideas about the Divine to keep me company. When peals of laughter wafted up to me, I opened my eyes. A raft was drifting downstream, its occupants specks of confetti at the bottom of the bluff. A leaf leapt from the end of a branch near my head. It swirled downward, until an updraft reversed its direction. Defying gravity, it disappeared into an oak that towered above me. Matthew's teaching rang true: the world was a magical display of my mind.

I'd hiked to the overlook along with a handful of residents from Sparrow Hawk Village, a community on the edge of the Ozark forest. Many of the locals were attending a meditation retreat that my husband was leading. I'd tagged along with him to enjoy the scenery and catch up on my writing. Then lingered on the ridge after my companions had returned to the village. Look at me, content, alone on a mountain trail—usually more at home in a mall.

The trail was well traveled. No fallen leaves obscured it, and the yellow blazes that marked it seemed superfluous. Offering more of a stroll than a hike, the path meandered through the woods, with an occasional uphill climb. It followed a ridgeline for half a mile, from the overlook to the village. I zigzagged around rocks that jutted up from the hard-packed earth. Then stopped to marvel at spider webs dangling from branches and saplings pushing up through the underbrush. After forty-five minutes, my feet hit asphalt. I was back in town.

The next morning, exhilarated and impatient to get back to the solitude of the trail, I tucked my phone into my pocket, saturated myself with bug repellent, and plopped on a baseball cap.

After arriving at the trailhead, I let the red blazes lead me back to paradise. They seemed farther apart than the day before. The flat trail presented no challenge. I hummed as I kicked through the drifts of leaves and stomped them with a satisfying crunch. At the third blaze, I glanced around, unable to see number four. But after squinting over the top of my sunglasses, I spotted it—too faint to show up through the charcoal lenses. I rushed over to it. A studious pan of the woods revealed only pristine tree trunks, no more blazes. I swept aside the leaves with my foot, hoping to uncover the trail. Nothing but underbrush.

This was crazy. Yesterday the path was hard, rocky, bare of vegetation. The blazes were... red? Yellow.

I had followed the wrong trail.

Hadn't gone far, just needed to backtrack.

I turned 180 degrees to locate the third blaze, spotted it, and exhaled a long sigh of relief. Careful to keep the sign in view, I trudged over to it and placed my hand on the swash of paint. The rough bark scratched, but its coolness slowed my quickening pulse. As still as the oak, feet planted to keep myself oriented in the right direction, I scanned the forest again.

The main trail should have been on the left. It followed the top of the bluffs parallel to the river, but there was no break in the tree line, which would indicate a ridge.

Maybe I got turned—

Blaze number two materialized; so distant I was surprised to spot it. I shivered, though the afternoon was warm.

I took off the cap, wiped my forehead with the hem of my tee shirt, then squinted in every direction. No blazes. Once again I reached out to touch the bark but snatched my hand away when a spider crawled too near. I twisted left, then right to create sightlines around the thickets. A sudden rustle through the underbrush caused me to jump. I squatted and softened my gaze. Was there a tramped down pattern in the carpet of leaves? No such pattern. No trail. A lizard ran across a log near my leg. I squealed, falling backward, and then scrambling to my feet. I put the cap back on. Tugged the visor down to block the sun, which glinted through the branches. My heart beat faster, louder. My mouth was dry. A paved road and a populated neighborhood lay only yards away. But which way? I looked behind me, searching for reassurance in the last blaze I'd passed, but the forest had swallowed it.

Just like me.

Adrenaline ripped away my breath. Smothered a nascent scream. The blood drained from my face, leaving me cold in the afternoon heat. I clutched my sides, lips parted, body rocking on the balls of my feet. My brain shut down. No daydreams, memory, or reason. I was pinned to the spot. Nauseous, clammy, and trembling.

A shroud of overhanging branches exploded in angry squawks that led to flapping wings and screeches overhead. Limbs creaked in the wake of the disturbance, as it faded from cacophony to hush, but a snap tore through the unsteady quiet when a branch broke off and crashed to the ground. A muggy breeze moaned through the canopy, while shadows loomed in the dense vegetation—a macabre dance across the trunks of trees that had closed ranks and stood shoulder to shoulder. No way through. No way out.

I gulped in a breath, inhaling a noxious mix of sweat, bug spray, and decaying leaves. I squeezed my eyes shut and massaged my neck until normal sensations crept back. Thirst. An itch. Reasoning power returned, along with a penchant for second-guessing. How long had I been out there? Should have brought water, should have noted the color of the blazes the day before. What a fool: not even knowing the difference between the bite of a fly and the sting of a brown recluse.

Memories flooded back. That people die of dehydration. That the locals found a hiker dead from exposure a few yards from her car.

Don't panic.

A new set of recollections. That the neighborhood was only five minutes away. That I'd stuck the phone in my pocket.

In one motion, I grabbed it and flipped it open. My hand shook, punching in Ben's number. When his voice mail came on as expected, I grinned at the sound of his recorded drawl. *Need to calm down, leave a coherent message.* But my voice was shrill with elation and relief.

"Hi, Honey. It's about noon. Help. I'm lost. In the woods. Close to a trailhead . . . don't know what direction... won't take long to find me. Following red blazes. Come and get me. Bye."

His phone would vibrate against his waist, so as not to disturb the hush in the meditation hall. He would check caller ID, listen to my message, and immediately organize a search party. In less than an hour they'd shout out my name and crash through the trees.

Safe. I loosened my grip on the phone. Nothing left to do but wait. I reclined against a tree trunk, hands folded across my belly. I turned my head from side to side to ease away the last bits of tension. A hundred feet to the left, a swipe of yellow stood out against the shades of gray and green.

Could that be—?

It had to be.

I reined in the urge to run, instead tromped through the ankle-deep drift of leaves, feet testing the ground for unseen roots. The hard-packed dirt of the main trail broke into view, as obvious as a six-lane highway.

I called Ben. "Honey, Honey. Cancel the emergency. Found the trail." I raced down the path toward the village. "Yay. Here's the street. Right where it should be. I'm so excited. Heading home. Love you. Bye."

I skipped-ran-walked down the block, anxious to tell my story. Lunch was winding down; time enough for a glass of ice water and a sympathetic ear. I craved human contact, nods of sympathy, hugs of concern. I opened the dining hall door, anticipating the murmur of conversation.

It was a silent retreat. No talking allowed.

I squelched my eagerness and slowed my pace to a mimic of walking meditation. An aluminum serving bowl held the dregs of a salad, a challenge to pluck out without clanking the tongs. I shook salad dressing onto the greens and carried my plate to the nearest table. A spattering of people sipped their last bits of tea as they deposited dirty dishes and tossed trash into the bin. One woman lingered, reading the bulletin board, before ambling out the door. A staff person emerged from the kitchen holding a push broom. With an occasional tap as the broom bumped a table leg, he swept away the remnants of lunch. Recollections of my fear and relief were already fading—scarves pulled from a magician's sleeve, set into flight with the flick of his wrist, only to settle at his feet. The entire adventure—nothing more than a magic trick.

The Road to Transformation

Ten Practices That Will Not Lead to Awakening

1. Affirmations

2. Yoga

3. Meditation

4. Mindfulness

5. Surrender

6. Prayer

7. Retreat

8. Reading spiritual books

9. Following a teacher

10. Forgiveness

Ten Practices That Might Not Hurt, You Never Know

1. Affirmations

2. Yoga

3. Meditation

4. Mindfulness

5. Surrender

6. Prayer

7. Retreat

8. Reading spiritual books

9. Following a teacher

10. Forgiveness

Resurrection:
Birth and Death Right Now

The graveyard beckoned me.

Matthew had assigned us to visit one, to contemplate the lives of the interred and reflect on the inevitability of death. My death.

I chose a cemetery in Parkville, a few minutes from home, discovered while running errands. Nobody familiar was buried there, but it seemed inviting and intimate. Mother Kim had used a cemetery as her walking track, drawn to the solitude. She would have liked this one, shady and deserted.

On the morning reserved to complete the assignment, I pointed the car toward Parkville but veered off instead, toward the hardware store. The day after that, the garden demanded weeding. A week later, the cleaners. But on an overcast spring afternoon, a cliché of a day, the cemetery beckoned me.

I pulled into the one-lane drive and parked.

Headstones, crumbling and skewed, clung to a hillside, which in turn sloped into a wooded area. Oaks bowed over those in repose. Leaves rustled in the breeze like prayer flags. I hoped it wouldn't rain but was grateful for the chill, glad to be alone.

I tramped through overgrown grass toward a granite marker. The inscription described the interred as a loving husband and devoted football fan. Its informality startled me. I scoffed. More exalted prose than that would certainly be needed to memorialize my years on earth. But then again, who was I to criticize? I was a devoted fan of beauty pageants.

The cemetery seemed an appropriate place to lay sarcasm to rest.

One row over, two seventeen-year-old boys were buried next to each other. They died the same year. Matching dates on twin monuments. A lump rose in my throat. Only babies. Returning home from the game or heading out to a party. Sons who'd no doubt left behind stunned mothers.

I was no different than those boys, as convinced of my immortality as any teenager. *Sure, I'll die some time, but certainly not today.*

A weathered headstone, the shape and size of an open Bible, caught my attention. It stood off by itself, listing like a ship with an unseen leak. The seasons had rounded its corners and smoothed its surface. In front of it, a pot of plastic flowers, blooms faded to gray, had fallen over. I bent down to set it upright.

"Margie Downing. Born 1926. Died 1961." An alternate spelling of my family name. Our name etched in the Book of Life. The stone bore no evidence of husband, children, or siblings. No other markers stood nearby. Margie Downing—dead at thirty-five, without a history and apparently alone.

That was me. Middle-aged. Neither wife nor mother. Destined for an untended grave. I felt lightheaded.

"Born 1926. Died 1961." Whatever had occurred between those dates lay buried among the bones. Pretty words that others might have inscribed—loving sister, devoted wife, faithful daughter—would only have been arbitrary scratches on stone.

Me—an arbitrary scratch on the earth.

With shaking hands, I righted the vase and then wobbled to my feet. Tears distorted the scene, the headstone growing until it loomed over the hillside and shimmered like concrete baking in the sun. My temples throbbed as the blood roared through my veins, drowning out the certainty that had regulated my life. Prior to the discovery of my name on a grave, I'd assumed that either accident or illness would cause my demise, but I was wrong.

Birth was the death sentence. I wasn't going to die; I was already dead.

Margie and me, meteors streaking across the void. The body in the ground mirrored the one standing over it. A single force animated both forms and observed itself through tearful eyes.

I staggered to the car, climbed behind the wheel, and waited for the mundane to restore my equilibrium. A woman hurried toward me, shouted "Sorry," and then re-parked one of the two cars I'd failed to notice had blocked me in. Automatically, although still weeping, I waved a thank you. The temporal and the eternal were as enmeshed as lovers.

Margie Downing haunted me, suggesting unexpected endings. She forced me to greet, wide-eyed, every newborn instant. In the days that followed, I became a phantom, gliding beside the life that used to belong to Dawn.

Saturday. I visited the farmers' market, intending to buy produce for the next week, but the sensation of having died would not reconcile itself with *next week*. I was compelled to simply absorb the crowded bazaar, where crimson peppers competed with golden peaches for my attention, and the aromas of ground ginger, cinnamon, and curry burst into the air like fireworks.

Tuesday. My sweetheart failed to set the plates on the proper rack of the dishwasher. Planning to confront him, I rehearsed my arguments. But Margie murmured no. From the vantage point of death, it was pointless to worry about dish racks. Ben's face, along with the words *I love him,* supplanted the aggravation. I was shocked, as though witnessing a miracle.

Wednesday. Reaching into the fridge for a bottle of water, I encountered a twinge of guilt and my father's long-ago voice. "Store-bought water's a waste of money. Just turn on the tap." His face had been twisted in derision. I wanted to soften those features, massage the corded muscles in his neck. *Rest in peace, Dad.* Margie and I toasted his memory. The cool drink tickled going down my throat.

Friday. I grew impatient when the grocery store clerk continued chatting. She left no pause where I could insert the final *thanks, bye.* My legs tensed like a runner's at the starting block. But hold on. I was dead—I had no deadlines to meet. I turned to face her. She recited a joke. We giggled. We commiserated about our gardens drowning under spring's deluge. She'd become as dear to me as an old friend, our relationship full and gratifying in sixty seconds. I left the store, ready to accept the next offer of friendship that might come my way.

Sunday. A spotless kindergarten boy nestled on the pew in front of me, between an elderly man and woman: he in a three-piece suit and she in a broad-brimmed hat. The couple intent as soldiers, while the little one—chomping on a piece of gum—inspected the ceiling, his shoes, and the underside of the gentleman's necktie. The youngster then removed the gum and inspected it. The lady withdrew a tissue from her purse and held it in front of him. Without a word between them, he deposited the glob. She stopped singing long enough to lean over and kiss her wiggly boy on the top of his head.

They handed me a secret treasure, but my body tightened around the gift. With that kiss, a rush of desire displaced the immediacy of death. I yearned to stretch the moment into perpetuity. Hold this sweetness.

After church, I sank into bed for a nap.

Existence in the physical realm brought fatigue... hunger... joy. Mop the floor, make love, mourn the lost—I didn't get to pick and choose. But every now and then, in split seconds glimpsed from a vantage point beyond the body, seen through the eyes of a phantom walking beside me, I no longer wanted to pick and choose. It was enough that each moment unfolded, fulfilled its promise, and flew into eternity.

It's an illusion to believe that death could happen right now. Death *is* happening right now. Resurrection follows.

The Inheritance

Day One. I didn't know if I was trying to outrun my history—or catch up with it.

Alone in a crowded student lounge, I waited for the Santa Barbara Writers Conference to convene. Other would-be authors filed in. Most meandered toward the registration table. Some relaxed in overstuffed chairs. Avoiding eye contact, shoulders tensed, I scanned the room for familiar faces. *Did they know Dad? Is that one of his students? Will anyone remember me?*

I'd grown up in Santa Barbara and then moved away. I hadn't returned in the ten years since my parents had died. Dad was a local hero. He'd taught at this conference for twenty years. He'd also published five books, authored 500 newspaper columns, and taught creative writing to 7,000 Santa Barbarans.

In the meantime, I had limped through high school and college, then dabbled in the careers of school librarian, fashion designer, hotel manager, university counselor, and hospital administrator. I'd resigned from the last position to become a writer.

Along the way, there were clues to an eventual love affair with the written word. As an undergrad, I preferred the essay question to the multiple-choice, the term paper to the final exam. Graduate school brought insight and the stirrings of a voice. My first research paper earned an A+ from my MA adviser. He added the comment, "You don't know how good you are." I flirted with prose in every job: sculpted memos into works of art, transformed newsletters into novels, reviewed dance productions for the hometown paper, and even proofed copy for classifieds. But I didn't notice the pattern. Like a haughty cheerleader pursued by the captain of the chess team, I didn't know writing existed until the day I ran away with it.

I quit my job to follow in Dad's footsteps. He would have disapproved.

I'm forty-one. After sojourns in Portland, St. Louis, and Minneapolis, I've landed in Kansas City. I've found the perfect job and call my parents to share the news.

"Dad, guess what?" He barely gets in a "Hi, Tootie," before I launch into my story. I pause for his congratulations.

He coughs from advancing lung disease. "I don't know why you keep quitting, but this job sounds good. I guess you're failing up."

I laugh along with him, but my cheeks burn, because I can't tell if he's praising me or mocking me.

CNN drones behind his wheezing.

Day Two. The leader of the morning workshop—a Fred Astaire type—stacked papers and books on a table at the front of the room. He wore sharply creased trousers and a crisp oxford shirt, with a cardigan draped across his shoulders. After introducing himself to the class, he strolled toward me. I averted my gaze from his face to the floor. His loafers advanced, stopping just opposite my sandals. I peeked at his knees. Then, raising my gaze and my courage, glanced at his belt buckle, and finally looked into his eyes.

He took my hand in both of his. "They told me you were coming. Your papa was a dear, dear friend. I miss him."

The breath I was holding escaped in a sigh. "Thank you. So do I."

I'm twenty-eight, home for the holidays. My teenaged sister and I are feuding. She sweeps past me to greet other family members with effusive air kisses. Wherever she stands, she turns her back to me. Her haughtiness reduces me from career woman to schoolyard victim.

After a day of toughing it out, I confide in Dad. We stand outside the front door. The night-blooming jasmine he'd planted along the driveway gleams in the moonlight. I tell him I'd rather spend Christmas with friends than endure that little shit's silent treatment.

"I wish you'd stay," he says. "You're not a quitter. I don't call you Snake Bite for nothing."

It's the only time he's called me Snake Bite.

He opens the door to encourage me back into the house. The scents of pine and cinnamon fill the living room. Seduced by this flirtation with his approval, I follow Dad inside and stay for Christmas.

Day Three. I broke the silence.

Other writers read their work aloud and bore up under the critiques. Their hands shook and their voices halted, while I hunkered down in the back of the room.

They'll find out I'm a fraud.

I imagined Dad's colleague embarrassed to discover his dear friend's daughter had no talent. When Mr. Fred Astaire read my name from his sign-up sheet, I interpreted his wry smile and the ironic lilt in his voice as *we'll just see what you can do, missy.*

I stood in front of the class and read an essay. The group

was supposed to offer suggestions, but no one spoke. I looked up from the page. They applauded. I gasped. It seemed polite to murmur thank you, but I wanted the clapping to stop. Surely I'd get into trouble for breaking some rule.

The teacher held up his copy of my composition. "You see," he said in that same clever tone, an eyebrow raised. "She did everything I told you to do in creative nonfiction."

I did? How did that happen?

The afternoon session had already begun by the time I located it on the sprawling campus. At first the room looked empty. The chairs had been pushed back against the walls, forming a semi-circle that faced a stool labeled the Hot Seat. One after another, participants perched there while they read a work-in-progress and listened to their colleagues' evaluations.

The facilitator directed the proceedings from behind a bare wooden desk. Reading glasses perched halfway down her nose emphasized her deadpan expression. After the class discussed chapter one of a memoir and the latest draft of a how-to manual, she tapped her roster with a pencil. "Dawn Downey is next."

Oh no, not me. My face grew hot and my hands cold, but I clutched my papers and stood.

I'm twenty. I stand at the sink, washing dishes. Dad sits at the kitchen table. He slouches in the chair with his legs stretched out. His size-twelve feet block the doorway. He studies my report card, which he holds in one hand, and then looks at me over his glasses. "You're failing."

"No I'm not. They're Cs, not Fs."

"Watch your mouth." His voice is low. It rumbles through the kitchen like a herd of buffalo stampeding over the plains.

I scour away at nonexistent grime in a skillet until Dad stalks out of the room.

The Hot Seat vibrated with menace. I willed my rubbery legs to move and crossed the expanse as though wading through waist-high mud. When I reached the middle of the room, a booming voice broke the silence.

"Dawn Downey? Bill's daughter? We lived up the street when you were in high school."

I turned to locate the source. A shout from the opposite corner rang out. "Bill's daughter? God, I loved that old man. I took his class six times."

The instructor frowned. She took off her spectacles. "Downey. I should have recognized the name. Your dad is the reason I'm here."

They converged on me. They hugged and patted and kissed. Their affection quelled internal voices that criticized and second-guessed. After cowering in the shadows for a lifetime, I basked in this newfound celebrity.

Order was restored, and I took my place on the Hot Seat. When I finished my recitation, someone yelled out, "You can't stop there. I've got to know what happens next."

The instructor held up her hand to prevent me from responding. "You'll just have to buy her book. Excellent work."

Maybe I *could* be a writer.

I'm eighteen. Dad drops me off at the Greyhound station. The brick building looms in front of me like Mount Doom. A bus labeled "Los Angeles" idles nearby. Exhaust blackens the air and stings my lungs.

I'm returning to college after a weekend at home spent begging my parents to let me quit. When they refuse, I plea bargain for a year off, and then a semester.

College life suffocates me. The co-ed dorms force me into unwanted intimacy with men I don't know. Stodgy literature professors suck the energy from Hemingway. The social pressure cooker that is 1970s Affirmative Action pits privileged white students from the suburbs against un-privileged black students from the inner city. As a middle class black girl, I'm trapped between the two factions.

Dad sends me back to a world where I'm lost, but his eyes are misty when he kisses me goodbye.

His tears embarrass me, as though I've accidentally seen him naked.

Day Four. I strained to hear my neighbor's voice above the din in the crowded cafeteria. Three of us had walked to lunch together and grabbed places at one end of a rectangular table. A group of conference staff—judging from the number of people vying for their attention—took seats at the opposite end. Isolated phrases broke through the surrounding racket. "... sales figures for my book." "... find the time to write my column." "... have to call my agent back." They represented everything I aspired to be. Popular, polished, published.

One of them picked up her chair and squeezed it in beside mine. "If it wasn't for your father, I wouldn't be a writer."

We sat knee to knee. As she leaned toward me, the noisy room receded. There was only the intensity of her gaze and the sweetness of her memory.

"When I came here as a student," she said, "I was scared to death. I took your dad's workshop because I heard he was friendly. On the last day, he asked, 'When are we going to hear from you?' I was too nervous to read my own work, but he talked me into it. I walked to the front of the room, shaking, close to tears. He leaned over and whispered, 'You're safe here.' And he held my hand while I read."

I was spellbound. Our mingled breath held her story aloft like a feather. As it floated away, she rose and returned to her group and the anonymity of clanking plates and pealing laughter.

He held her hand while she read.

A stranger had just revealed that my father was Superman, and his secret power was tenderness. Maybe, if I'd known his identity before he'd died, Superman would have held my hand, too.

I'm sixteen. Dad and I sit with his boss, the editor of the *Santa Barbara NewsPress*. Our three chairs form a tight circle.

I propose an article for the paper: race relations among high school students. I rattle off prospective interview questions for my classmates. I read my synopsis, stumbling over the power of the two men beside me. Intimidation halts my speech. Excitement propels me.

The editor nods while I talk. He smiles at me, then turns to Dad. "What do you think, Bill?"

Dad folds his hands in his lap. "I wish I'd heard about it before now." His words press in on my chest.

My heart races. "Sorry, Dad." I study my feet. "Sorry."

I feel him next to me like a rock face I can't possibly scale.

The editor's comments drift by. "Flesh it out." "Meet again." They grow fainter as the room fades away and I disappear.

Day Five. Dad's former students caught up with me as I entered buildings, emerged from restrooms, and strolled down walkways. Messengers from my father, they shared the words of encouragement he'd written across their manuscripts. Some had continued to meet for a decade after Dad's death, reserving an empty seat for him at the head of the table. They recited his pithy advice. "Take more risks." "Write outrageously." They repeated phrases unfamiliar to my ears. "I'm proud of your progress." "Just incredible." They unveiled my inheritance: Dad's

Technicolor self-portrait, which I'd only seen in shades of gray.

I'm ten years old, lying in the bow of his cabin cruiser. We've been fishing, just the two of us. He sits on the deck smoking his pipe. Vin Scully is calling a Dodgers game on the radio. Mosquitoes buzz. Lightning bugs flicker. The river rocks me to sleep.

Day Six. I juggled a plate of fruit and a glass of orange juice as I navigated around the buffet table at the closing brunch. Luggage and tote bags left little space for walking. The ballroom resounded with shouted compliments and promises to email. There were flurries of exchanged business cards.

After finishing the meal, we settled in for the awards ceremony. Every announcement of someone else's accomplishment felt like a personal failure. From disappointment I descended into guilt, for my lack of generosity. The inner turmoil distracted me, until the sound of the family name yanked my attention back. "… Downey… first prize… creative nonfiction." A tablemate poked me in the ribs, while another squeezed my shoulders, assuring me I'd heard correctly. I grinned so hard my cheeks hurt as I made my way to the stage.

I'm six years old. Dad sits on the step stool in the kitchen, holding a jar of pickled pigs' feet. I climb onto his lap. His big arms surround me as he reaches into the jar and offers me a bite. The tangy taste plays hopscotch on my tongue. Dad grins. I swing my legs.

When I reached the stage, the conference founder presented me with a certificate and kissed me on the forehead. I read my winning essay aloud at the pace of chocolate melting in my mouth. I savored this bit of success at the craft my dad loved. The spotlight's glow made up for all the years I'd felt invisible. When I took my bow, students whom my father had encouraged and teachers he had taught applauded my achievement. They nodded their approval. Invisible arms wrapped around me and I knew Dad's hand held mine.

I'm fifty-four. My father beams. "Incredible, Snake Bite, just incredible."

Light and Shadow

I should have been a better daughter.

On the night Kim Carol married Dad and became my stepmother, Mama forced me to go to the wedding. She shoved me, a morose fourteen-year-old, out the door and into my uncle's car, along with my three siblings. I'd longed to stay home with her. It would have been just the two of us; maybe then she'd have noticed me. But without offering an explanation, she ordered me to go. Then she turned and scuffed up the stairs, the hem of her bathrobe raising a wake of dust bunnies.

Aunts and grandmothers gossiped that Mama was lazy. "Catherine's been that way," they said, "ever since her father's deathbed accusation. He claimed she told the authorities about his bootleg operation."

I didn't understand what any of it meant, but if I'd been a better daughter, she would have gotten over being lazy. She would have brushed my hair, read me stories, and sung away my nightmares. We would have planted marigolds together.

Those moments, however, played out only in my imagination. By the night of that wedding, I felt worthless, unnecessary. I might have died for lack of a good reason to live, had Kim Carol not married Dad.

Maybe that's why she died, thirty years later.

The oncologist said the lump in Mother Kim's breast was the biggest and oldest he'd ever seen. A ghostly silhouette on the mammogram. She refused to explain why she'd let it go untreated. Hinted that she didn't mind dying, and besides, she was busy taking care of her mother-in-law. Her poetry left clues behind, like breadcrumbs on a path.

Two bits
My pocket said
As it opened a hole
And spent my dreams.

I didn't understand Mother Kim while she was alive, but if I'd been a better daughter, I would have mended that pocket.

I learned how to love my two mothers long after they were gone. I had become a hospice volunteer, looking for meaning in the deaths of strangers, since none was found in those losses closer to home. The search ended on a summer afternoon, with the revelation that what I'd experienced was more precious than what I'd sought.

Squinting into the August glare, I climbed the front stairs of a suburban ranch house and rang the bell. When Mr. Murphy answered, the sun danced across his smiling face, spilling into the entry hall behind him. The local hospice had assigned me to sit with his wife—bedridden and lost to Alzheimer's—while he ran errands.

He glanced over his shoulder toward the rear of the house. "I think she's awake today."

Passing through a living room sprinkled with family photos, he ushered me into the den. Picture windows on three of its walls framed a manicured back yard. Sunshine poured in. Cushions printed in violet and lime plumped up a white wicker couch and ottoman. *Better Homes and Gardens* lay on a matching table. The furniture had been pushed aside to accommodate a hospital bed. Approaching it, I felt uplifted.

The room bore no resemblance to the grief-shadowed space where Mother Kim had spent her last nights. Cancer had shrunk her sweater-girl figure until the king-sized bed dwarfed her. Sun peeking in through half-closed blinds had painted narrow stripes across her sunken face.

Mother Kim hadn't liked stripes. She'd lived in splashes of color: crimson lipstick, turquoise jewelry, purple dresses. She had even worn green ruffles at her wedding.

After they were married, she and Dad bought a home on the other side of town and filled it with his four teenagers. Nobody told us why we no longer lived with Mama Catherine in our old house. But the odors of mildew and dog droppings that had clung to that life were slowly displaced by Pine-sol and Chanel No. 5. My new mother fixed hot cereal for breakfast. She came to parent-teacher nights. She painted the dining room red. I breathed her in like a drowning woman gulping air.

Mrs. Murphy's bed faced a television set tuned to a country music video station. When I leaned over to say hello, she smiled up at me. Her unlined face and pixie haircut belied the degeneration reflected in her toothless grin.

"Are you going to do my hair now?"

"She thinks you're the beautician that comes every week," Mr. Murphy said.

I played along. "I'd love to do your hair."

"Expense?" she asked.

"Nope. I'm free."

Mr. Murphy pushed the controls that raised the head of the bed. The motor whirred until his wife sat upright.

She frowned.

He reached for a glass on the bedside table. "Want some water, Honey?" Leaning down to her, he touched a plastic straw to her thin, cracked lips, his words more croon than question.

My memory searched for tender moments shared with either of my mothers. None surfaced. Waking nightmares haunted me, instead.

Dad moved his family across the country. Birthdays, graduations, and Christmases passed without visits or phone calls from Mama Catherine. I could not exhume the sound of her voice. She wrote letters, which I neither saved nor remembered. They were postcards from a stranger.

Her absence festered, its significance unacknowledged, like the tumor in Mother Kim's breast.

When I was a single twenty-something, my stepmother and my sister Michelle knocked at the apartment door. They looked grim and hesitated before they stepped across the threshold.

"Dawn," Mother Kim said, "your mother has died."

What are you talking about? You're standing right here.

It took a second for the pieces to fall into place. Mama Catherine had suffered a heart attack. Michelle hugged me and talked about arrangements.

If I'd been a better daughter, I would have gone to the funeral.

Years later, I took care of Mother Kim during the last weeks of her life. By then Dad was dying, too. Early one morning, pain broke through her medication. She labored under the effort to breathe. Her lungs, like bellows, fueled cancer's fire with each inhalation. I phoned the doctor and waited an endless hour for his service to call back. They told me to contact our hospice nurse.

Mother Kim sat rigid as a corpse at the kitchen table. Her eyes were closed, her lips pursed.

More calls, more waiting.

A nurse arrived with morphine. She plumped a vein. It didn't respond. She tried another. "I'm so sorry, Kim." She raised the other arm. Poke, press, plump. No veins. All collapsed.

I couldn't bear to watch. I couldn't turn away. Words of comfort stuck in my throat. Hands that should have stroked her hair hung useless at my sides.

The nurse retrieved a child-sized needle from her car. It slipped into the vein.

Mother Kim bit her bottom lip. Her face relaxed as a morphine haze crept over her.

Although the ordeal seemed to end at dinnertime, she woke up moaning in the middle of the night. Dad was cough-snoring in front of the television down the hall.

The sound of my mother's need was insistent. But, lying in bed in the room next to hers, I turned away from the sobs and stared at the moonless sky outside the window.

Mr. Murphy gave me instructions and headed off to the grocery store.

I suspected my companion was uncomfortable. "Would you like the bed adjusted?

She nodded.

I plucked the switch from under the covers. Reading glasses perched on my nose, I fumbled with the device. "Is that better?"

Her frown remained.

I pressed the buttons again, and the head of the mattress retreated. "How about that?"

"Better."

I leaned over to straighten the bedclothes, studying her face for signs of distress. There was no strain in her expression. No pursed lips.

The television blared a beer commercial. I turned it down, then parked myself on a stool next to the bed. "Thanks for letting me visit you today."

She studied the ceiling. "Where's my coat? I'm going home."

"Can you can stay a little longer?"

"I have a job."

"Yes, and you're really good at it."

It was a game of follow-the-leader. She weaved in, out, and around our chat, while I skipped along behind.

I patted her leg—barely discernible among the pillows and blankets. "Where are you in there?"

We both chuckled, sharing the cosmic joke.

Our voices drowned out the demons that shrieked in the background of my life.

Mother Kim told her journal she "... never did close well, except with babies and old people..." In fact, she collected them. When I was in high school, she cared for four children kindergarten-age and younger—my brother and sister, my niece, and a foster child. When they grew up, even though cancer had begun its march, she took in my grandmother and another toddler from the next generation.

"God," she asked in a poem, "if you wanted me so soon, why'd You leave another child saying I love you Grandma?"

I remained one of her babies through high school. I was a sullen teenager, but she would not leave me to my sulking. She bought me a hot pink party dress. Introduced me to *Wuthering Heights*. Waited up until I returned home after dates.

I called her Mother for the first time on the day she and Dad drove me to college. From the back seat, I gawked at my future unfolding outside the car windows.

"I think the dorm's over there... Mother." I tested the sound of it, drew it out to feel it vibrating in my throat. Muh-ther. It felt like riding a bike for the first time, and I was glad to get out of the car so we didn't have to talk about it.

My college years must have been the leading edge of that time warp between "babies and old people," because that's when she closed *in*, instead of closing *well*.

On a Friday night when I was home from school she said, "We're going on a liquid protein diet together. You'll lose five pounds this weekend. Won't that be great?"

I only weighed a hundred. Independence was what I lost.

She had saved my life, but then kept it for her own purposes. If I had been a better daughter, maybe she'd have set me free.

After she came down with pneumonia toward the end of my sophomore year, she asked me to come home to help her. I left school a month before the semester ended, and although I thought the American Lit professor had approved my absence, he scratched a red F on the grade sheet at the end of the term. I reported to his office the following autumn.

"You didn't turn in your papers," he said. He shook his head and questioned my priorities. "You missed too many classes."

I worried the corners of the tablet in my lap. *You don't understand. Mother called.*

After I graduated, she took me to get a driver's license. It became the ball at the end of my chain. I chauffeured her. To thrift stores, where she shopped for grandchildren whose parents' thank-yous engendered unsolicited advice about the right way to raise children. To the mall, where she fingered designer dresses in her size and walked out empty-handed.

To the grocery store, where she second-guessed every bunch of broccoli before placing them in the cart. She carried no credit card or ID, only a couple of folded checks, which she excavated from the bottom of her purse.

She tapped her pen on the counter, while the clerk called the manager. "I was just here two weeks ago. Why do we have to go through this again?"

I waited by her side, fidgety. *If I do this, maybe it will be enough.*

At the same time the local university hired me, Mother Kim became a secretary in the English department. I drove her to work every day. Filing did not suit her. "It's so left-brain," she said. She wrote poetry whenever her boss left her alone in the office.

I was in charge of the chancellor's schedule, in the days of pencil-and-paper calendars. The morning was overrun with phone calls to and from the assistants to department heads. We were coordinating timetables to accommodate an emergency meeting. "Hmm... 11:30 will work if I can move his lunch with the student body president. Let me call you back."

My office-mate waved at me. She pointed to the blinking light on her phone. "A lady wants you. Tried to get her name, but she refused to say."

"Hello? This is —"

"Who's that awful woman?"

"Muh-ther—"

"Why does she need to know my business?"

"That's what she's—"

"Anyway, how do you spell *mesmerize*?"

If I do this, maybe it will be enough. "M-e-s..."

I was thirty, lying beside my boyfriend on his bed. Lights off, incense burning. His phone rang. He answered and then handed the receiver to me.

"I don't know what to do about your sister."

"What—?"

"Is this a bad time?"

"How did you even get this number?"

"Oh, are you on a date?"

I married him, and we moved to a different state. But every summer, I resumed chauffeuring.

In between visits, a pattern developed. *I should call home.* The guilt intensified until it was almost unbearable—almost. Our phone rang; it resounded with a hint of annoyed edginess.

My husband picked it up. "Hello? Yeah." And then pointed the receiver in my direction.

I asked her if she wouldn't mind saying hi to him before asking for me. "You'll like him. Really. He's got impeccable manners," I said, as though *his* actions needed a defense. "He just doesn't know it's you."

"I've got impeccable manners, too."

She didn't call back for five years.

Following the cancer diagnosis, I phoned to check on her. Dad answered and caught me up on her condition.

"Can I talk to her?"

"Toots wants to know how you are, Kimmy."

"Sick of answering that question. That's how I am."

Dad and I had a tacit agreement—he would not let her die before I got to see her again. *Not this one, too.* Our calls ended in a well-practiced exchange.

"Do you want me to come home?"

"No, we're okay. There's nothing you can do."

Until the time the phone rang seconds after I'd hung up.

"I don't know," he said. "Maybe you should come on home."

Cancer was a complicated thing. Doctors, drugs,

documents. Dad had grown too ill himself to handle it. So I became the manager of my mother's death.

I refilled her lapsed prescriptions, hired aides, drove her to the cancer center, stuffed the refrigerator with the food dropped off by friends, got her great-grandson off to preschool.

"Why did you come back?" she asked.

"I didn't want you to die with us not talking."

If I'd been a better daughter, I would have been kinder.

I wanted to say *I love you... don't leave me.* To her? To Mama Catherine? Hoped she—they—would say it back. We were facing each other, sitting on twin beds pushed against opposite walls in the guest room. A spider made its way along the baseboard. I felt as awkward then as the day I'd first called her Mother. I still didn't know how to ride that bike.

The sun streamed through Mrs. Murphy's windows, warming me as I perched on the stool beside her bed. When the growling in my midsection signaled snack time, I reached into my bag for an apple. "Do you mind if I eat?"

"We used to have a big back yard," she said.

"We did, too, with roses and oranges and avocados. And apples so sour, they scrunched your mouth." I made a face at her. "Only Mother and I liked them."

"Did you bake pies?"

I crunched the Granny Smith. Its tartness bit my tongue. "Gosh, no. I'm not great in the kitchen."

Mother Kim had encouraged me to maintain a high-powered career and a Scarlett O'Hara waistline. She hadn't gotten around to teaching me domestic niceties. We'd pored over *Vogue*, not *The Joy of Cooking*. But she'd stared at me wide-eyed when, at age thirty, I bumbled around the stove. "You can't even make spaghetti? How do you feed your husband?"

If I'd been a better daughter, I'd know how to cook.

Mrs. Murphy's eyes were closed. The hesitant rise and fall of her chest hinted at the waning of life. I stroked the hair along her temple with the backs of my fingers.

The stillness of mid-afternoon enfolded us and sheltered me from the busyness of my world. Tempted by the couch's thick cushions, I curled up and lowered my eyelids in meditation. My mind sank into tranquility, undisturbed by the thoughts that drifted through it. When the darkness behind my eyelids brightened, I checked to see if the sun had emerged from behind a cloud. The light in the room remained unchanged. I closed my eyes again. Once more, a sudden brilliance. A second peek still revealed no difference, and my curiosity faded, leaving me in a state both restful and alert. Mrs. Murphy's breathing rustled across the room. A sofa button poked into my back. Isolated sentence fragments winked inside my mind before sinking back into nothingness.

After meditation ended, I was oddly content, as though understanding a problem I'd been puzzling over, but not connecting the feeling with anything in particular. Blinking through my haze, I walked over to check on my companion.

She still dozed, breath even. After I poured myself a glass of water in the kitchen, I returned to find her staring at the ceiling.

"Did you have a good nap?" I asked.

She replied without missing a beat. "We both did."

"Boy, that's the truth. You're a great nap partner. When can we do it again?"

She did not hesitate; her voice was steady and strong. "Tomorrow."

Hide and seek. She—concealed in the thicket of Alzheimer's. Me—giggling whenever she popped out. I wanted to go another round, but the front door opened, and Mr. Murphy brought in the groceries.

I met him in the kitchen, heard about the prices of soup and baby food, and then returned to her bed to say goodbye. She'd disappeared again, off to play in other realms. I started toward the door but turned to face her once more.

She startled me with an expression that was alert, a gaze as deep as Einstein's. I was transfixed. I breathed a sigh of relief, as though finding my way after being lost. I had the sense of remembering, without knowing what had been forgotten. The sensation of recognizing a departed friend, without knowing where or when we'd ever met. I stood beside her, silent. Her eyes reflected mine, and mine hers, back and back through the ages, until there was neither a she nor a me.

I stroked the translucent skin of her cheek. Melting ice clinked in the glass on her table. Country music twanged softly from the television as I smoothed the blankets around her. A cabinet door creaked shut in the kitchen.

"Thanks for keeping me company," I said.

She said... nothing.

It was enough.

At the precipice of life, with a gaze of piercing tenderness, Mrs. Murphy freed me.

I was enough. No need to be a better daughter. It was enough to be.

I, in turn, freed Catherine and Kim Carol from the need to make me whole. They were enough.

I'd sought the one's affection in the swamps of *why* and the other's in the caverns of *should*. Why-don't-you-notice-me versus why-don't-you-leave-me-alone. One mother's dead air, the other's static—they carried no more relevance than the chatter of child's play.

The warp and weft of conversations with a woman I knew

for only a day revealed that words did little to illuminate love. It sparkled, instead, in the brilliance of a gaze, the shimmer of a giggle, and the flicker of a caress. It was a shove out the door toward a brighter life.

At the end of the search, I didn't find meaning. Love rendered it moot.

I kissed my fingertip and touched it to Mrs. Murphy's brow. Walking through the kitchen, I exchanged goodbyes with her husband, stepped into the afternoon sun, and closed the door behind me.

About the Author

Downey's essays have been published by *The Christian Science Monitor, Shambhala Sun, Skirt! Magazine, Kansas City Voices: A Periodical of Writing and Art,* and *The Best Times.* Her work is anthologized in *Alzheimer's Anthology of Unconditional Love: The 110,000 Missourians with Alzheimer's, My Dad is My Hero: Tributes to the Men Who Gave Us Life, Love, and Driving Lessons* and the *Cuivre River Anthology.* Her writing has earned awards from the Missouri Writers Guild, Oklahoma Writers Federation, Northern Colorado Writers, and the Santa Barbara Writers Conference.

From the first day azaleas bloom until the night black-eyed susans give in to a hard freeze, find her on the patio, tending a container garden. She lives in Kansas City with her husband, Ben Worth. He spoils her rotten. She reciprocates.

If you enjoyed *Stumbling Toward the Buddha*, sign up here to receive a new essay in your in-box every month: DawnDowney.com/Newsletter

Connect with the author online at:
DawnDowney.com
DawnDowneyBlog.com
Goodreads.com

Acknowledgments

The author gratefully acknowledges the publications where the following essays first appeared:

Alzheimers Anthology of Unconditional Love: a shortened version of "Light and Shadow," titled "She's Awake"

Kansas City Voices: A Periodical of Writing and Art: "Alone in the Dark" and "The Inheritance"

Pooled Ink: Celebrating the 2012 NCW Contest Winners: "The N Word"

Shambhala SunSpace: "Truth Transcends the Facts"

Skirt! Magazine: "Mirror, Mirror"

Poetry quotations in "Light and Shadow" are taken from the chapbook *Some Days I Can't Get My Underwear On* by Kim Downey.

Thank you to friends, colleagues, and loved ones.
My spiritual teacher, Matthew Flickstein
Developmental Editor/Coach, Marcia Meier
Copyeditor, Julie Tenenbaum
Kansas City Writers Group
WTF Writers Group: Jessica Conoley, Karin Frank, Teresa Vratil, Dane Zeller, and the late Bob Chrisman.
And to Uncle Al and my siblings for their memories and encouragement: Allen Downey, Sr., Michael Downey, PhD, Michelle Downey Lawyer, William Downey, Jr., MD, Wayne Downey, EdD, and Leslie Downey Moorman.

www.ingramcontent.com/pod-product-compliance
Lightning Source LLC
Chambersburg PA
CBHW032039290426
44110CB00012B/868